NativeSpain.com

GOING NATIVE IN CATALONIA

Simon Harris

NativeSpain™.com

First Published in Great Britain 2008 by www.BookShaker.com

Typeset in Trebuchet

GOING NATIVE IN CATALONIA

For Magdalena Amorós i Mena...
my first guide to Catalonia

Praise for this book

'I have been to both Barcelona and the Costa Brava on a number of occasions, and I had always said to friends and family that I was going to Spain. After reading this book, I am not only more enthusiastic about going back but I will also have a much better idea about where I'm going and will definitely consult a Catalan phrasebook before I leave.'
Martin Fullbright, Cheltenham

'We have a lot of English-speaking visitors to our company, and I have often wondered how I could tell them about Catalan culture in a way that they would understand. This book is the perfect answer to my problem. Well done!'
Núria Santacreu, Barcelona

'I've never seen my part of Barcelona even mentioned in a guide book before!'
Paul Fisher, Nou Barris, Barcelona

'Very helpful. It gave us an insight into the way things are done that would have been difficult to pick up from anyone else.'
Jean Grandy, Tossa del Mar

'Quirky, crazy and a lot of fun. I found myself laughing out loud at some of the observations because they rang so true.'
Pete Osborne, Badalona

Contents

Overview

INTRODUCTION

With a coastline that stretches 700 kilometres from the rugged Costa Brava on the French border passing through the Costa del Maresme and the city beaches of Barcelona right down to the golden sands of the Costa Daurada in the province of Tarragona, it is not surprising that Catalonia is a prime destination for tourists from all over the world – but the Principality offers the visitor much more than just its beaches. Skiing holidays in the Pyrenees, a weekend break in Barcelona or rural tourism in the Ebro Delta are obvious alternatives, and the diverse geography of the region along with its history, architecture and vibrant sense of its own culture make any stay in Catalonia one to remember. I should know I came here on holiday more than twenty years ago and still find living here a continual delight.

Modern Catalonia is the rump of a Mediterranean nation that included Valencia, the Balearic Islands, Rosselló in the south of France and the independent state of Andorra, and an empire that incorporated Sardinia, Corsica, Sicily, Milan and Naples, and for a brief period stretched as far as Greece and Asia Minor. Although remnants of Catalan dominance can be found all over the Mediterranean, in the present day, the Principality is now restricted to the top north-eastern corner of the Iberian Peninsula.

Given their impressive imperial history and their cultural and linguistic differences from the rest of Spain, the Catalans have long considered themselves an independent nation within the Spanish state, and from a geographical point of view it is easy to see why this is so. The Principality is clearly defined by the Pyrenees to the west, the Mediterranean to the east while the River Ebro forms its southern boundary separating it from neighbouring Valencia. Its northern border, however, allows easy access into France, with whom it has close historical and linguistic ties. So, while cut off from central and southern Spain by the Meseta, Catalonia is a 'terra de pas', a passageway, that links the mysteries of Iberia with northern Europe, and its geographical position explains much of its turbulent history.

Catalonia has a cultural flavour that is markedly different from southern Spain, and this is particularly evident both in its Gothic and Romanesque architecture and in the cadences of the Catalan language. One of the reasons for this is that both architecturally and linguistically, Catalonia received very little Moorish influence. The Moors began their conquest of the Iberian Peninsula in 711, but never really succeeded in controlling Catalonia, and the reconquest of Girona in 785 and Barcelona in 801 meant they never had time to leave their mark. This is in sharp contrast to the rest of Spain where their dominance lasted centuries, with the 'Reconquista' by Ferdinand and Isabella not being completed until 1492.

To this day, Catalan territory is divided along the lines established by the Franks and Catalan Counts in the 8th and 9th centuries. The comarques, of which there are 41, are similar to the English counties. They have their own identity based on geography, agriculture and commerce, and are governed by a district council made up of elected municipal members. However, for administrative purposes within the Spanish state, since 1833, the Principality has been split into the four provinces of Barcelona, Girona, Lleida and Tarragona.

The Principality is one of the largest of Spain's 17 Autonomous Communities covering an area of some 32,000 square kilometres, making it bigger than many other countries in the European Union including Belgium, and with a population of around 7 million, Catalans comprise about one sixth of all Spaniards. The region is also economically prosperous, and, in Barcelona, boasts a capital that is on a par with any other major European city

Just as in the rest of Spain, the Principality has a regional government with its own President and Parliament. However, after the end of Franco's dictatorship, the Generalitat was 'restored' in 1977 whereas the other autonomous governments were not created until 1979 when the new democratic constitution was ratified by the Spanish Parliament. The Catalans are quite rightly very proud of their political institutions and democratic traditions. *Els Usatges*, for example, is one of the first documents to define the rights of the people and the obligations of their rulers, and predates the English Magna Carta by almost 150 years.

For long periods of their history, the Catalans have pushed for independence from Madrid. However, with the passing of Catalonia's updated Statute of Autonomy in 2006 and a new Statute in Andalusia this year, Spain in the 21st century is becoming increasing federal. Now Catalonia's cultural and linguistic rights are safeguarded, calls for complete independence are becoming less frequent, and what's more... living in such a beautiful, diverse and prosperous country, who on earth would want to complain?

A BRIEF HISTORY

Though Catalonia has formed part of Spain for nearly 300 years, Catalans only grudgingly admit the fact. Current relations with distant Madrid are as good as I can remember, mainly because socialist President José Luis Rodriguez Zapatero has a very positive attitude towards the Catalans and their culture, and consequently treats them with the respect they deserve. However, his right-wing predecessor José Maria Aznar, who was Spanish President until 2004, was a different matter altogether. During his presidency, continual snipes at the Catalans including a proposal to impose the Spanish humanities and languages syllabus in Catalan schools and a ludicrous plan to divert the River Ebro south before it reached Catalonia brought back the ghost of Franco in many people's minds. The Principality has suffered too many periods of repression at the hands of the Spanish for the Catalans to ever completely trust Madrid.

It was a dreary day and the banks of the Ebro were close to bursting, so the effect of this river memorial to 35,000 dead in the Civil War was even more sobering.

Catalonia's independent streak is also justified by more than 2,000 years of history. When the Romans came to the peninsula, more than 200 years before Christ, they divided their newly-conquered territory into two; Hispania Citerior, which roughly corresponded to modern Catalonia, and Hispania Ulterior, the rest of the peninsula. Tarraco, present-day Tarragona, was the capital of Roman Hispania and when Emperor Augustus made the city his home in 26 BC, it was briefly the capital of the whole of the Roman Empire.

FOUR FINGERS OF BLOOD

Legend has it that whilst still a vassal of the Carolingian emperor, Guifré el Pelós (Wilfred the Hairy) Count of Barcelona was wounded in battle against the Moors. The appropriately named Frankish king, Charles the Bald, realised that without their leader the Catalan troops would be much less motivated on the following day. He grabbed a golden shield, plunged his fingers into Guifré's wounds and wiped them across the surface of the shield. The next day, the Catalan troops went into battle under the standard and won the battle. This flag, depicting four red stripes on a yellow background, is now the Senyera – the Catalan flag.

The Making of Catalonia

In 711, the Moors crossed the Straits of Gibraltar and swept through the Iberian Peninsula. They captured Barcelona in 717 and then crossed the Pyrenees and went as far as Poitiers before being checked by the Franks. In desperation the inhabitants of what was to become Catalonia turned to Charlemagne, the powerful Frankish leader for help in return for pledging allegiance to the Carolingian Empire. Girona was retaken in 785 and Barcelona in 801, and the province of the Spanish March, a buffer zone between Christian France and Muslim Hispania, was born.

The Spanish March was governed by local counts, who had political and judicial functions but were ultimately responsible to the Frankish king and were appointed and could be dismissed by him. The most powerful of these counts was Guifre el Pelós who managed to unite the counties of Urgell, Cerdanya, Girona and Barcelona, and so controlled a swathe of land that stretched from Barcelona to Perpignan along the coast and inland to the Pyrenees. It was Guifre's son, Guifre Borrell, who became the first hereditary ruler of Catalunya Vella, Old Catalonia. The next step on the road to nationhood came in 985 when the Moors, under Al-Mansour, managed to cross the River Llobregat and conquer Barcelona. The Catalans called on the Franks for help but received no military support. Consequently, Count Borrell II declared independence, and although this was not recognised by the Franks until 1258, an independent state called Catalonia was born.

The next two centuries were spent consolidating their territory and pushing the Moors south towards the Ebro, and in 1137 Count Ramon Berenguer IV married Petronella, the infant daughter of the King of Aragon. His son, Alfons I, became the ruler of the most powerful state in Southern Europe, the Catalan-Aragonese Confederation, which consisted of Catalonia, Aragon and the whole of the south of France. With considerable help from the Knights Templar, the Moorish threat became a thing of the past.

Under Jaume I the Conqueror (1213-1276) the Catalans sought to drive the Moors out of the Mediterranean completely. During his reign, Catalonia conquered Mallorca in 1229, Ibiza in 1235 and Valencia in 1238. Furthermore, aware of the need for dialogue between the sovereign and his subjects, he instituted the Corts, a consultative body in which the three classes of the nobility, the clergy and the urban bourgeoisie were represented. Over the next century Mediterranean expansion continued with the conquest of Sicily, Sardinia and Southern Greece, including Athens, and the democratic processes were increased with the founding of the Diputació del General, initially a tax collecting body which was later to become the Generalitat, the government of Catalonia.

CATALAN TERRITORY

If you have any doubts about how far Catalan influence extended, and still extends to this day, you could ask yourself why a French Rugby League based in Perpignan in France, which competes in the SuperLeague and recently disputed a Cup Final against St. Helens, calls itself the Catalan Dragons. Similarly, you might be interested to know that for 80 years during the 14th century, the Parthenon in Athens was known as La Seu de Santa Maria – southern Greece had been conquered by the Catalans, and giving such an important monument a Catalan name was a sign of the Catalan empire's power. Furthermore, in Sardinia, where the people still speak a Catalan patois, when someone doesn't express themselves well, they will be told 'No sidi su gadalanu' – literally, 'He doesn't speak Catalan'.

The Death of a Dynasty

Just when Catalonia's Golden Age was at its height, disaster struck the House of Barcelona. In 1410, Martí the Humane died without heir and Fernando de Antequera, second son of Juan I of Castile, was elected king of the Catalan-Aragonese Confederation. As Castilians, he and his successors had little knowledge of Catalonia's rule by consensus. They rarely visited their kingdom and imposed Castilian legislators who managed to incite the people so much that civil war broke out during the reign of the tellingly named Joan II Without Faith. Things got even worse when Fernando II, who had married Isabel of Castile in 1469, acceded to the Catalan-Aragonese throne. He immediately introduced the Inquisition, expelled the Jews causing an economic crisis, insisted that his subjects proved they had no Arab blood, and even though, after discovering America, Columbus had sailed into the port of Barcelona, Fernando and Isabel prohibited Catalonia from trading with the Americas.

Spaniards claim that the reign of the Catholic Kings marks the beginning of Spain as a nation. However, although from the reign of Carlos I onwards the Catalan-Aragonese Confederation was ruled by the same monarch as Spain, technically it was still an independent state with its own laws, and when it traded with the rest of the peninsula customs taxes were levied.

During the reign of Felipe IV, the monarch came under the influence of the autocratic Count-Duke Olivares, who when war broke out with France in 1635 demanded a disproportionate contribution of money and men. Since, according to her constitution, Catalonia should only pay those taxes which had been approved by her own government, the answer was a firm no. So, determined to bring his rebellious subjects into line, Olivares launched a campaign into France across the Pyrenees from Catalan territory in which 10,000 men who had been recruited against their will were slaughtered. Not satisfied with this sacrifice, he then billeted Castilian troops in Catalonia, who, in the true spirit of friendship, raped and robbed the locals. The situation came to a head in 1640 when the reapers, who gathered in Barcelona to work on the harvest, revolted, burned down government buildings and murdered Felipe IV's Viceroy. The destructive 19-year Guerra dels Segadors, the three-way Reapers' War involving Castilian, French and Catalan troops ensued, and in the Treaty of the Pyrenees in 1659, Felipe IV ceded all Catalonia's French territories to the French Crown. Medieval Catalonia had ceased to exist.

Things went from bad to worse when Felipe IV's son, the half-wit Carlos II, died without heir in 1700. There were two pretenders; the Bourbon, Philippe de Anjou, grandson of Louis XIV, and the Habsburg Archduke Charles of Austria. Castile favoured the former while Catalonia the latter and, after allying with England and Holland, who feared a French-Spanish axis, welcomed him to Barcelona as Carles III of Catalonia-Aragon in 1705. The war of Spanish Succession broke out, and just when all seemed to be going well, the Archduke's brother died and Carles was called back to Vienna to be crowned Holy Roman Emperor. To the English and Dutch a united Austria and Spain was as unpleasant a prospect as a French-Spanish axis, so they pulled out of the alliance leaving Catalonia alone to face 200,000 Franco-Spanish troops.

The Breaking of Catalonia

The Catalans held out well considering the odds against them, but on 11th September 1714 Barcelona finally fell after a long siege, and Felipe V's retribution was devastating. The Generalitat and the Council of One Hundred were disbanded, Catalonia's ancient rights and privileges were abolished and speaking, reading or writing in Catalan became an imprisonable offence. All of Catalonia's universities were closed and replaced by the heavily-censored government-controlled University of Cervera. The Ciutadella, a huge fort, was built in Barcelona along with new city walls, which were designed not to keep invaders out but to keep the people in. Catalonia had ceased to exist and the Catalans had become the lost nation.

Although Catalonia's great literary tradition would be completely lost for the next century, the Catalans never stopped speaking their own language, which simply went underground and was spoken in secret, and being a canny lot, their economy was soon on its feet again. Now officially part of Spain, the Castilians could no longer excise customs taxes on Catalan products, and Catalan cotton, leather and wine, in particular, began to flood the Spanish market. Aware of the Catalans manufacturing skills, Carlos III allowed the Principality to trade with the Americas in 1778, just in time for Catalonia to take advantage of the Industrial Revolution. The economic boom was so successful that, with its cotton and textile industry at the forefront, Barcelona became known as the 'Manchester of the Mediterranean'.

Economic success brought increasing confidence and by the early decades of the 19th century, the Catalan language came out of hiding and began to be spoken in public again. The turning point came in 1833, however, when Bonaventura Carles Aribau, who funnily enough was working for a bank in Madrid at the time, published 'Oda a la Pàtria', a poem that spoke of the homesickness he felt for his homeland. Although of dubious literary quality, the poem was written in Catalan and was so popular in Catalonia that it soon sparked a flood of imitators. These imitations slowly developed into a fully-fledged literary movement known as the Renaixença, and by the mid 19th century

Catalan poetry, prose and theatre were in as good a state as they had been 150 years earlier. The booming economy and literary Renaissance also brought the first rumblings of a new Catalan political consciousness. Catalans began to believe that they were every bit as good as the Castilians.

FREEDOM FIGHTERS

Just behind the church of Santa Maria del Mar in the barri of La Ribera in Barcelona, there is an unassuming little square called El Fossar de les Moreres. It was here that the leaders of the resistance against Felipe V's troops were lined up against the church wall and shot in 1714. There is an eternal flame and a plaque, which reads:

Al fossar de les Moreres
No s'hi enterra cap traïdor.
Fins perdent les nostres banderes,
Sera l'urna de l'honor.

In the cemetery of the Moreres
No traitor is buried.
Even though we've lost our flags,
This will be their urn of honour.

Like a Phoenix from the Ashes

It was in Castile that the next step on Catalonia's road to political recovery would be taken. Tired of centuries of absolutist misrule, which for most Spaniards resulted in abject poverty, many began to see Catalonia as an example to be followed. So when the First Spanish Republic was declared in 1873, it was not surprising that the first two Presidents of the Cortes in Madrid were Catalan. Although the short-lived republic only lasted a year, this brief period of freedom of expression allowed politicians from other Spanish regions, such as Galicia and the Basque Country, to consider the idea of federalism. These ideas did not disappear with the restoration of the monarchy, and as the century reached its close, a young Prat de la Riba formed the bourgeois Catalanist party, the Lliga Regionalista.

By 1906, the Lliga Regionalista had gained the support of Republicans, Socialists and Carlists as a respectable bourgeois group that could strengthen the cause against Monarchists and against the workers and their anarchist fringe. In 1914, Madrid decided to grant Catalonia some concessions, and the Mancomunitat, with Prat de la Riba as President, was set up. Although it was early days to re-establish the Generalitat, the Mancomunitat of Catalonia was a regional administrative body financed by local taxes, with its seat in the Palau de Generalitat in Barcelona.

Given Barcelona's anarchist history, it's not surprising that the anti-globalisation movement has taken root. 'Occupy' and 'Resist' read the graffiti on the roof of this squat just below Gaudí's Parc Güell.

The early decades of the 20th century were far from peaceful. The plight of industrial workers and the disaffected poor in Barcelona was taken up by the Anarchists and left-wing Trades Unions with often violent consequences such as the Setmana Tragica, the Tragic Week, of 1909 during which the streets of Barcelona exploded into street fighting and church burning. The whole of Spain was divided between Republicans and Monarchists, but at least Catalonia had gained a modicum of autonomy.

When Miguel Primo de Rivera staged a military coup in 1923 and installed himself as dictator of Spain, disbanding the Mancomunitat and illegalising the Catalan language once again, the divisions in Spanish society were deeply drawn. Primo de Rivera's dictatorship lasted until 1930, and after a brief return of the monarchy, the 1931 General Election returned Spain's ill-fated Second Republic. The stage was set for civil war.

With support from Madrid and the working classes in Catalonia, Francesc Macià, the President of the Generalitat, declared the Federal Republic of Catalonia on August 2nd 1931. Two years later a General Election returned a right-wing government in Madrid, which disbanded the Generalitat and called on General Franco to violently put down a miners' strike in Asturias. On October 6th 1934, the left-wing lawyer Lluís Companys declared the Autonomous State of Catalonia and he and his government were imprisoned. The Spanish General Election of February 1936 was won by the Popular Front, a left-wing coalition, and in Catalonia Esquerra Republicana, the Catalan Republican Left, won a landslide victory, even though its leaders were still in prison. Two weeks later, they were released and Spain's President Azaña reinstated the Generalitat and the 1932 Statute of Autonomy. On July 18th 1936, General Franco and four other chiefs of staff launched a military coup against the democratically elected Spanish Government. The Spanish Civil War had begun.

The Civil Guard policed the countryside and their slogan *'Todo por la Patria'* - *'Everything for the Fatherland'* can still be seen all over Catalonia. Just a remnant of a history of oppression?

In Catalonia, the armed uprising against the Republic was rapidly suppressed by workers' militias and the Civil Guard, who remained loyal to the Generalitat. There was a lot of infighting amongst loyalist troops, and the Communists finally ousted the Anarchists as the main political and military force in Catalonia. Early in the war, the Spanish Government fled Madrid, first to Valencia and then to Barcelona, so the Catalan capital was effectively capital of Spain for a brief while. Things finally came to a head in the autumn of 1938 when the Catalans stood alone at the Battle of the Ebro against the Nationalist troops, who were aided by their Fascist allies, Italy and Germany. After months of fighting and many deaths, the Fascists swept across the Ebro and Barcelona soon fell. The Spanish Civil war officially ended on March 28th 1939 and on April Fools' Day of the same year, Franco declared 'peace' in Spain.

From Dictatorship to Democracy

The Generalísimo was particularly anti-Catalan, and as soon he was in power, he imprisoned, tortured and executed thousands. President Lluís Companys was captured by the Nazis in France, returned to Hitler's allies in Spain and duly executed on Montjuïc in 1940. Catalonia suffered a period of political, linguistic and cultural repression, which remains the shame of the 20th century.

By the 1950s, illegal Catalanist groups began to take their first tentative steps towards organising an underground resistance. By the 60s, Abbot Escarré of Montserrat, who as a religious leader was under the protection of the Vatican, began to stand up to Franco and act as a focus for moderate Catalans. In 1974, the clandestine Assemblea de Catalunya, in preparation for Franco's death, came out into the open under the slogan 'Liberty, Amnesty, Statute of Autonomy'.

When Franco died on November 23rd 1975, all sections of Catalan society were ready to take control of their destiny again. On September 11th 1976, the Catalan National Day, a million and a half people took to the streets. In 1977, President-in-exile, Josep Tarradellas, came back to lead the restored Generalitat, and a new Statute of Autonomy was passed a year later. On March 20th 1980, the democratically-elected Catalan Parliament formally opened under the Presidency of Jordi Pujol, leader of the Catalan conservative party, Convergència i Unió.

El Gran President, Pujol, led Catalonia from dictatorship to democracy, while the Socialist Mayor of Barcelona, Pasqual Maragall, set about repairing the damage done to the Catalan capital. In 1985, Barcelona won the nomination for the 1992 Olympic Games and, in the run up, the city was covered with the slogan 'Barcelona, Posa't Guapa' – 'Barcelona, Make Yourself Beautiful'. The Olympics were an incredible success and were seen by all Spaniards as an example that the New Spain should follow.

In 2003, Pujol retired and Maragall took his place as President. With the Socialist José Luis Rodriguez Zapatero as President of Spain, there was a government in Madrid sympathetic to Catalonia, and a new Statute of Autonomy was passed in 2005. This allowed the Catalans to describe themselves as a 'nation within the Spanish state' for the first time in nearly 300 years, and with another socialist, José Montilla, elected president in 2006, the future looks bright, The Lost Nation has found itself once again.

THE COLUMBUS MONUMENT

Not surprisingly, Christopher Columbus is a source of some pride for the Catalans who, although he was Genovese, often claim him as one of their own. These claims shouldn't be taken desperately seriously, though, because they call him Colón, which sounds like a part of the lower intestine to me. They've also built a monument to him at the bottom of the Les Rambles in Barcelona. Admittedly, he **is** pointing out to sea in a very conquistatorial fashion, but in actual fact his finger is pointing towards Libya, not South America. Nobody can be expected to get it right all the time!

Timeline

- 100,000 BC – The approximate date of a Homo erectus jawbone found at Banyoles in Northern Catalonia. However, flint and other remains suggest that the region has been populated for around a million years.

- 10,000-500 BC – Berbers move up the Levante coast from Africa, Basques cross the Pyrenees and Celts come down from Central Europe. Separate tribal societies are formed, and the coastal tribes begin to trade with other Mediterranean peoples.

- 800 BC – The Greeks arrive first at Roses and then later at Emporion (modern Empúries) on the northern Costa Brava. The towns are little more than trading posts and the Greeks only have cultural influence over the tribes in their immediate vicinity. They do, however, coin the name Iberians that many centuries later would be applied to the whole peninsula.

- 218 BC – The Romans oust Hannibal and his Carthaginians from Catalonia and make their capital first in Empúries and later in Tarraco, modern Tarragona. They divide the Peninsula into two: Hispania Citerior (more or less modern Catalunya) and Hispania Ulterior (the rest of the Peninsula).

- 200-100 BC – The Romans build the Via Augusta road, which connects Southern Spain with Rome. The political and cultural process of romanisation is completed.

- 27-26 BC – The Roman emperor Augustus settles in Tarraco making it capital of the Roman Empire for a brief period.

- 20-15 BC – The Romans establish a small settlement called Barcino, which would later grow into the great city of Barcelona.

- 300 AD approx. – Germanic tribes begin to invade and challenge Roman hegemony over the Iberian Peninsula.

- 460 AD – The Visigoths take control of Catalonia making Barcelona their capital. They later gain control of the whole Peninsula and move their capital to Toledo.

- 711 AD – The Moors invade the Iberian Peninsula and conquer territory as far north as Poitiers.

- 759 AD – The Franks, under Pepin the Fat, retake Rosselló and move south reclaiming Girona in 785 and Barcelona in 801. The borders of Catalunya Vella are established south of the River Llobregat.

- 870 – Guifre el Pelós becomes first Count of Cerdanya and Urgell. He later takes control of Girona, Osona, Besalú and Barcelona. On his death in 897, the Countship of Barcelona and its vassals becomes hereditary and the Catalan nation is born.

- 897 - Guifre el Pilós is killed in battle against the Moors. Legend has it that the Catalan flag, La Senyera, is created when the Frankish King wipes four fingers of Guifre's blood across a golden shield.
- 985 – The Moors attack and control Barcelona but are driven back South within a couple of years. Lack of military support from the Franks provokes the Catalans to declare independence.
- 1060 – The establishment of the Usatges de Barcelona. This primitive document, which outlines the rights and responsibilities of the (free) people, predates the Magna Carta by more than 150 years and gives Catalunya a reasonable claim to be the 'Mother of Democracy'.
- 1112 – Catalunya extends its influence over the south of France through the marriage of Ramon Berenguer III to Dolça de Provence.
- 1137 - Ramon Berenguer IV marries Petronella of Aragon and the Counts of Barcelona become Kings of Aragon.
- 1148 – The Conquest of Tortosa and Lleida.
- 1213 – Pere the Catholic is killed at the Battle of Muret defending his Cathar subjects against the forces of Simon de Montfort and the Catholic Church. Catalunya's influence in the south of France is reduced to Rosselló.
- 1229 – Jaume I better known as the Conqueror begins the conquest of Mallorca, to be followed by Ibiza and Formentera in 1235 and Valencia in 1238.
- 1282 – Pere II the Great conquers Sicily. Catalonia is now the most powerful Mediterranean empire.
- 1287 – Alfons II conquers Menorca.
- 1302-1311 – The Catalan mercenaries, the Almogàvers, begin expansion into Greece and Asia

Minor, culminating in the conquest of Athens and Neopatria.

- 1352 – The Generalitat is founded, and Sant Jordi (St George) is declared patron saint of Catalonia.

- 1410 – Martí the Humane, the last of the Catalan dynasty, dies without heir.

- 1412 – After the Compromís de Casp, Ferran d'Antequera, of the Castilian Trastàmara family, is elected King of the Catalan-Aragonese Confederation.

- 1443 – The conquest of Naples.

- 1479 – Fernando II of Barcelona and Aragon marries Isabel of Castile. The foundations for what will become the Spanish state are laid.

- 1492 – Columbus returns to Barcelona after the discovery of the Americas and the Moors are finally expelled from the south of the Peninsula.

- 1516 – Carlos I becomes the first Habsburg King of Spain, and declares that Catalonia cannot trade with the New World so driving the Principality's economy into decline.

- 1556 – Felipe II becomes King of Spain, converts the village of Madrid into his new capital and bans any Catalan trade with the Americas.

- 1640 – After a century of marginalisation, the Catalans take up arms against the Spanish state and the 19-year-long Guerra dels Segadors (The Reapers' War) begins. In the peace, the Spanish government hands over Northern Catalonia to France.

- 1700 – After the death of Carlos II without heir, the Spanish War of Succession begins between supporters of the Habsburg and Bourbon pretenders. Catalonia allies with England and Holland and backs the losing Habsburgs.

- 1714 – On 11th September, Barcelona finally falls to the Bourbon troops and the new King, Felipe V, exacts his revenge by revoking Catalan laws, illegalising the Catalan language and building the Ciutadella fortress and walls to keep the Catalans under control.

- 1737 – Foundation of the first textile factory in Catalunya. The industrial revolution has arrived.

- 1778 – Catalunya is allowed to trade with the Americas.

- 1793-1814 – A series of wars between France and Spain leave Catalonia weakened. In 1807, Napoleon occupies the Principality and offers to create an independent Catalan state.

- 1848 – The Barcelona-Mataró line is inaugurated and becomes Spain's first railway.

- 1840s – Following its economic growth, Catalunya begins to rediscover its language and culture which blossoms in the 'Renaixença'.

- 1860s – The people of Barcelona demolish the Ciutadella and the city walls; plans are begun for the expansion of the city with the building of the Eixample.

- 1888 – The Universal Exhibition heralds the arrival of a new architectural style known as 'Modernisme'.

- 1892 – The Bases de Manresa are drawn up outlining a Republican plan for Catalan autonomy.

- 1909 – Barcelona's workers rebel against being conscripted for Spain's war against Morocco, and a week of street violence and church burning ensues. The week is known as the Setmana Tragica, the Tragic Week, and hints at the grassroots at the strength of feeling that would be harnessed by the far left and the Anarchists in the following decades.

- 1923-1930 – Miguel Primo de Rivera takes over as dictator of Spain. The Catalan language is outlawed and Catalonia suffers another period of harsh repression.

- 1929 – Barcelona hosts its second Universal Exhibition and work on the Barcelona Metro begins.

- 1931-1934 – Francesc Macià declares the Republic of Catalonia and the Principality receives a degree of autonomy within the Spanish state. Lluís Companys becomes President of the Generalitat in 1934.

- 1936-1939 – After an attempted coup by Franco's Nationalist rebels, the Spanish Civil War begins. Barcelona holds out almost to the end briefly becoming the seat of the legitimate Republican government, but finally falls after the Battle of the Ebro during which the Fascists received military aid from Hitler and Mussolini.

- 1939-1975 – During Franco's dictatorship, the Catalan language and culture is violently repressed. The Generalitat continues in exile under the Presidency of Josep Tarradellas.

- 1950s-1960s – Spanish immigrants flood Catalonia in search of work.

- 1960s-1970s – The tourist boom begins to transform the Catalan coast.

- 1975 – Franco dies and Prince Juan Carlos is appointed King of Spain.

- 1977 – The Generalitat is restored and in October Josep Tarradellas returns to become its first President with the prophetic words 'Ja soc aquí' – 'I'm here now'.

- 1980 – The first democratic elections are held and Jordi Pujol is elected President of the Generalitat, a position he maintains until his retirement in 2003.

- 1992 – Barcelona hosts the hugely successful Olympic Games. The damage of the Franco years begins to be repaired.
- 2004 – José Luis Rodriguez Zapatero, a socialist sympathetic to the claims of Spain's stateless nations, is elected President of Spain.
- 2006 – Catalonia's new Statute of Autonomy is passed giving the Catalans the right to call themselves a nation.

JOSÉ MONTILLA

Perhaps the clearest example of the fact that Catalonia is a place where anyone can build a life and succeed comes in the figure of the current President of the Generalitat, José Montilla. Born in Córdoba in Andalusia, Montilla came to Catalonia as a boy along with many other impoverished Andalusian immigrants. The fact that he is now our President is a testament to the plurality and openness of the society in which we live.

PEOPLE AND THEIR QUIRKS

It's impossible to give an accurate view of the character of a people in just a few words, because it inevitably leads to stereotyping. However, when you look at how a nation describes itself, it is possible to give an idea of how it wants to be seen.

The Catalans are a proud self-confident people, who describe themselves in terms of *seny*, which means something between common sense and fair play. When asked to give you examples of this they will say that they are practical and hard-working, and cite Catalonia's economic success as proof of this. Although fiercely nationalistic at times, most of them tend to take their lack of independence philosophically and so haven't resorted to the violence of their sister nation, the Basques. Their capacity for dialogue and debate means they value their thousand-year democratic tradition, and are confident that they will achieve the degree of autonomy they desire by political pressure, they are often stubborn but *seny* occupies a central role in their attitude to themselves and the world around.

The flipside of this is *rauxa*, a kind of good-humoured gay abandon that is so typical of Catalan festivals or the celebrations that occur after Barça win a major football title. Obviously, all work and no play is very dull, so the Catalans' sense of fun is almost feverish. Parties are 24-hour affairs, but despite the crazy excesses, both sexual and chemical, the idea is to enjoy oneself. People drink, hug each other, and let off fireworks with an almost innocent joyousness that is so endearing. No-one knows how to party like the Catalans.

Unfortunately, the rest of Spain doesn't share the opinion the Catalans have of themselves. I was giving a class on the subject of National Stereotypes recently, and after having a bit of a laugh at the expense of the Germans, French and Americans, I asked them what they thought of the British. They were quite categorical; we're polite, reserved and very bad at cooking. Given that there were a couple of Spaniards in the group, I thought it best not to get into the sensitive subject of what the Catalans think of the rest of Spain, so I decided to turn my attention onto the Catalans themselves. Typically, the adjectives that are proffered are intelligent, honest, hard-working etc, but this day was a little different, and everybody was a little taken aback when a businessman from Seville blurted out, 'Mean and unfriendly'.

In general, Catalans don't get a very good press in the rest of Spain, and are often described using the very same words; mean and unfriendly. Although completely inaccurate, this stereotypical view does reflect the deep cultural differences between Catalans and Spaniards.

With the powerful seaport of Barcelona as its capital, Catalonia has long been a centre of Mediterranean trade and commerce. Not surprisingly, this means that the Principality has traditionally been wealthier than the rest of the peninsula, and so sour grapes are probably the reason why they are considered to be mean. They are also much less ostentatious than Castilians, and unlike in Madrid, tend to dress down and give the impression that they've got less money than they actually have. Furthermore, the tradition of 'inviting' isn't part of Catalan culture, and people are much more likely to pay for their own drinks and food rather than flamboyantly paying for everyone else's. However, with good friends that I drink with frequently, we often end up paying for rounds secure in the knowledge that, over time, everything will come out in the wash. So whilst not being overtly generous, it's unfair to say that the Catalans are mean.

Similarly, when it comes to making friends, the Catalans function much as I do myself; they take their time. One of the things I find most irritating about other Spaniards is the way they want to be your best friend within the first five minutes. They buy you a drink, are fascinated by the English and will soon be inviting you to their home (and, unfortunately, themselves to yours). However, within a few days they'll be flitting off to charm someone else into an ephemeral friendship. This has happened to me so many times in the last 20 years, but although I have many Spanish acquaintances I can't count one amongst my 'real' friends. When a Catalan invites you into their home, however, you know you've got a friend for life.

So what do I like about them? Well, I suppose it's their gruff directness combined with a very dry sarcastic sense of humour that, having been born and brought up in the north of England, makes me feel so at home here. I was recently chatting with a Mancunian colleague at the British Council in Barcelona, who like me often has difficulty minding his ps and qs in an over polite environment. 'It's bad enough coming from Manchester' he said, 'but after twenty years with the bloody Catalans, I'm even worse.'

I suppose another thing I like is that you have to function on their terms, which oddly means that they are one of the least prejudiced peoples I've ever encountered. They don't care about race, colour or creed; where you came from and the purity of your blood is not a consideration here. If you bother to learn the language and understand the culture, you will be accepted as a Catalan on full terms. The ex-President of the Generalitat, Jordi Pujol, once said 'Any man who speaks Catalan to his children can consider himself a Catalan'. People who continue to only speak English or Spanish and are always harping on about how much better everything is back home will get the cold shoulder, though. But that's not so unreasonable, is it?

The point is, that it's up to you how much you want to get involved. If you play by their rules, you will be completely accepted as one of them. I, however, still remain a little reticent at times. This is because, amongst themselves, they are incredibly clannish and group-oriented. They dance in circles. They build human castles. They form groups and societies for just about everything; to sing, to play sport, to discuss politics, study nature and go on excursions. Once accepted you will be invited to form part of the circle, and it's this that I find difficult. I'm an individualistic Anglo-Saxon lone wolf, and so I don't always want to be part of things. It is not then the Catalans supposed unfriendliness that is the problem, but my own.

EL RUC CATALÀ

Given that bullfighting isn't part of the culture here and that most people find the macho image of the black 'Toro Bravo', the Spanish bull, vaguely repulsive, the Catalans needed an animal to identify with. You'll see bats and dragons all over the place but a few years ago a couple of teenagers from Banyoles hit on an idea for a car bumper sticker that all Catalans are proud to show off. El Ruc Català, the Catalan donkey, is the complete antithesis of how Spain wants to represent itself. Although critics claim that the donkey is a stupid animal, Catalans see it as hard-working, gentle and honest – the perfect image of *seny*.

LANGUAGE

Many foreigners who visit or come to live in Catalonia are either unaware of the importance of the Catalan language or are worried that their minimal Spanish will not be understood by the locals. There is no cause for concern. Most Catalans are bilingual, and are surprised when they encounter a non-Catalan with a good working command of the language – although around 10 million people speak Catalan, they are well aware that in comparison with 400 million Castilian-speakers, theirs is a minority tongue.

Since the passing of the Spanish Constitution in 1979, both Castilian and Catalan are official languages in

Catalonia, and given that the Principality is a magnet for tourists, the Generalitat is investing considerable resources in the teaching and learning of English. Catalan children begin their English lessons aged four in most schools, and there are plans to stipulate a minimum level of English competence before university students can obtain their degrees, so Catalonia's linguistic future looks bright.

At the moment, though, you will normally have to 'get by' in Castilian. Apart from in the remotest villages, this should be no problem, as four out of the six major television channels that can be seen in Catalonia broadcast in Castilian to the whole of Spain, and the flood of immigration from the south that began in the fifties means that many 'New Catalans' grew up speaking Castilian at home. However, out of politeness, it is not a bad idea to learn a few basic expressions. These should provoke a broad smile in recognition of the fact that you are making an effort, and if you are eating out in a Catalan (*però molt Català*) restaurant, you might get slightly better service. I will include some basic vocabulary in a later section, but *Si us plau* (*Por favor* in Spanish) meaning 'Please' would be a good place for any visitor to begin.

Catalonia has suffered long periods of repression by the Spanish State, and apart from brutality and political violence, the target has often been the language. Catalan was first banned in 1714, when Philip V annexed Catalonia, and it was prohibited again under the dictatorships of General Miguel Primo de Rivera (1923-1929) and General Francisco Franco (1939-1975). The language is robust and flexible with a strong literary tradition, and although Catalans could be arrested for speaking it in public, the police state never managed to eradicate it from the private world of the home and family. However, even though Spain has been a democracy since 1979, many older Catalans are unable to read or write in their mother tongue as their schooling was conducted completely in Castilian.

Franco was particularly anti-Catalan, and his propagandists claimed that the language was nothing more than a dialect of Castilian. This fabrication was part of the fascist rewriting of Spanish history, and ignores the fact that the two languages developed from different roots, albeit both of Latin origin. When the Romans conquered Spain, they divided it into two provinces – Hispania Citerior comprising of modern Catalonia where Vulgar Latin dominated and Hispania Ulterior consisting of the rest of Spain where principally High Latin was spoken. The result of this is that Catalan has as much in common with French and Italian as it does with Castilian Spanish. A few examples should make this clear.

In literary Latin, the word *metus*, meaning 'fear', gives us *miedo* in modern Castilian, whereas the Vulgar Latin word *pavor* results in *por* in Catalan, *peur* in French and *paura* in Italian. Similarly, *comedere* is the root of *comer* in Castilian which means 'to eat', and the relationship between *manducare* and the words it spawned is obvious when we look at the Catalan *menjar*, the French *manger* and the Italian *mangiare*. If we are aware that phonetic changes in Castilian have often led to the substitution of h for f, it is easy to see from where *hablar*, the Castilian verb meaning 'to talk', derives – in High Latin it is *fabulare*. The Catalan, French and Italian words, *parlar*, *parler*, and *parlare* respectively, however, are rooted in the Vulgar Latin term *parabolare*.

Furthermore, Catalan is a pure Latin language with no Arabic sounds, unlike Castilian which was influenced by the Moors for 800 years, meaning that around 15% of

Castilian words are of Arabic origin. For example, all Spanish words that begin with 'al' (*alcachofa* – artichoke, *alfombra* – carpet) have an Arabic root and the expression *Ojalá* meaning 'If only' is the contraction of an Islamic oath. In contrast, Catalan has much more in common with northern European languages, and if you can get to grips with its complex grammar and pronunciation system, it is actually easier to pass for a native Catalan than it is to pass for a native Spaniard. Barcelona taxi drivers, for example, who can only see my Anglo-Saxon complexion through their rear view mirror, have often mistaken me for a Catalan born and brought up in another part of Catalonia.

My mate Edu is the proud driver of one of the few Hackney cabs in Barcelona – if you should be lucky enough to get a ride with him, make sure to give a big tip!

The language is full of short sharp sounds like *cap* for 'head', *fill* for 'son' and *clau* for 'key'. Many verbs are similar – *crec* for 'I believe', *vaig* for 'I go' and *vull* for 'I want'. These words make the Catalans sound brusque and direct, in comparison with their flowery and romantic Castilian neighbours, and there is an element of truth in the jibe that if you just say the first half of the Spanish word and keep a grim expression on your face, you'll find yourself speaking Catalan. However, Catalan pronunciation is more varied than Castilian which only has five vowels sounds – a, e, i, o, u – whereas Catalan has a myriad of possible vowel pronunciations. It also has diphthongs just like English does. To get a feel for it, my advice is to listen, listen, listen.

There is an element of truth in the jibe that if you just say the first half of the Spanish word and keep a grim expression on your face, you'll find yourself speaking Catalan.

So if you are coming to Catalonia on holiday, you don't need to bother learning Catalan. Similarly, if you come to live here and spend most of your time with other ex-pats, you will be able to get by in Castilian. However, if you want to live and work with the Catalans and expect to make friends with them, you will find that you can only go so far without learning their mother tongue. They will be polite if they know you don't speak Catalan and do their best to address you in Castilian, but if you work in an office or go out with a group of them, you really cannot expect them to speak to each other in a foreign language just because you cannot be bothered to learn theirs. How do we British feel about immigrants who spend years in our country without ever gaining a good command of the English language? The Catalans are quite a lot more tolerant than we Brits, but at the end of the day, the choice is yours – it all depends on the extent to which you want to integrate into Catalan society.

If you decide to take the plunge and get to grips with this beautiful ancient literary language, you have lots of options available. No fewer than 18 UK universities teach Catalan language and literature, generally as a sub-department of the Spanish or Hispanic studies departments. A full list is available on the Anglo-Catalan Society website at *www.anglo-catalan.org/lectors.htm*

In Catalonia itself there are many options for learning the language. La Escola Oficial d'Idiomes has branches throughout the country with the main one in Barcelona being at Avinguda Drassanes s/n (tel. 93 329 2458) at the bottom of the Rambles. Other possibilities are the Centres de Normalització Lingüística (*www.cpnl.cat*) whose head office is in Barcelona at Pau Claris, 162 (tel. 93 272 3100), or private language schools such as International House. Furthermore, there are several Catalan courses that can be followed online at *www6.gencat.net/llengcat/aprencat/recursos.htm*

Language Links

www.anglo-catalan.org/lectors.htm
www.cpnl.cat
www6.gencat.net/llengcat/aprencat/recursos.htm

CATALAN IN ENGLISH

You might be surprised to find that a few words with Catalan origins have made their way into English. My favourite is the word 'cul-de-sac' meaning no-through road in English. In Catalan, it means the bottom, or more literally the 'arse', of a bag. There's also the word 'llaut', a medieval fishing boat which has become 'yacht' in English and has been re-exported to Catalan as 'iot'.

Other words that were coined in Catalonia are 'liberal' and 'guerrilla', to describe the flash attacks that the Catalans made on Napoleon's forces during the Peninsula War.

CULTURE

When you look back at Catalonia's rich artistic and cultural heritage, it's not surprising that Barcelona has become one of the style capitals of Europe. For more than a thousand years, the Principality has managed to pull in European and Mediterranean influences whilst somehow making them magically its own.

Catalonia's earliest definable architectural style was Romanesque, which resulted in the building of nearly two thousand churches and monasteries between 1000 and 1250. You can almost trace the Christians' victories over the Moors by observing its architecture. In the northern Pyrenean enclaves, such as the valleys of Boi and Aran or the small town of Ripoll, the churches are smaller and mesmerisingly simple showing strong French, or more accurately Frankish, influence. As the conquest moved further south and Barcelona's confidence as a Mediterranean seaport grew, the scale of religious architecture also grew in stature. Monasteries, such as those at Poblet and Santes Creus in the Province of Tarragona, are more ambitious and show overseas influence, particularly from Lombardy in Italy. The even more ornate Lleida Cathedral is another example of late Catalan Romanesque.

Given the sheer number of Romanesque buildings, the key to discovering architecture from this period is to get off the beaten track and explore the inland villages. Particularly in the north, these churches were once sumptuously decorated with murals and frescoes, but by the end of the 19th century vandalism and the elements had deteriorated them so much that they had to be saved. Using a process known as strappo, they were removed from their original sites and can now be viewed at the Museu Nacional d'Art de Catalunya

(MNAC) on Montjuïc in Barcelona and the Museu Episcopal in Vic.

Both these museums also contain wonderful collections of Catalan Gothic art, which date from the late 13th to the early 15th century. Examples of this architectural style can be found in Barcelona, which in the Barri Gòtic contains one of the best-preserved medieval city centres in Europe. Most of the government buildings around Plaça Sant Jaume date from this period, whilst Santa Maria del Pi and the breathtaking Santa Maria del Mar are also not to be missed. Similarly, Girona Cathedral, which Gaudí cited as one of the essential buildings on the Iberian Peninsula, is truly awe-inspiring.

Following the death of the Catalan royal lineage and the accession of a Castilian to the throne in 1412, Catalonia entered a period of political and economic decline, which was accompanied by a lack of artistic creativity. Consequently, the Renaissance and Baroque architecture is not on a par with Catalan Romanesque and Gothic. However, examples can be found, and a walk down Carrer Montcada in Barcelona will bear witness to this. For the later Imperial styles that followed Catalonia's annexation by Spain in 1714, you should visit the Catalan Parliament building in the Parc de la Ciutadella or the University of Cervera.

By the mid-19th century, economic prosperity triggered by the Industrial Revolution also engendered a cultural revival, first in literature and music and later, in the run up to Barcelona's 1888 Universal Exhibition, in architecture. This movement known as Modernisme was a Catalan Art Nouveau, which fortuitously coincided with the expansion of Barcelona's city centre into the Eixample. With over a thousand Modernist buildings, the style is one of Barcelona's trademarks, but the work of the three great masters Lluís Domènech i Montaner

(1850-1923), Antoni Gaudí i Cornet (1852-1926) and Josep Puig i Cadafalch (1867-1957) and their collaborators can be found in the most unlikely corners of Catalonia. Much the same as with Romanesque and Gothic, the trick is to get off the beaten track and explore.

The Modernists were so prolific that it is impossible to catalogue their work in this short introduction. However, you can compare and contrast their styles on the Manzana de la Discordia, the Block of Discord, on the corner of Passeig de Gràcia and Carrer Consell de Cent in Barcelona. Within just a few metres of each other, you can observe the work of these three great iconoclastic architects.

Gaudí's dragon just above the entrance of Parc Güell has become one of the symbols of the city of Barcelona and of the Catalan people.

Perhaps the least appealing of the three, at Passeig de Gràcia, 35 is Domènech i Montaner's Casa Lleó Morera. His other masterpieces include the Palau de la Música Catalana and the Hospital de la Santa Creu i Sant Pau. A few doors up at number 41 is Puig i Cadafalch's striking Casa Amatller, while the most extraordinary is the Casa Batlló, next door at number 43, by Gaudí, who is of course world famous for the Sagrada Familia, Parc Güell and Casa Milà, better known as La Pedrera.

By the beginning of the 20th century, Modernist architecture also heralded in a parallel movement in visual art. This group of Paris-influenced artists, poets and musicians was led by Ramon Casas, whose work can be seen at the Museu d'Art Contemporánea in Barcelona, and Santiago Rusinyol, whose private studio, the Cau Ferrat, is now a museum in Sitges. However, to get a real feel for the times, you should visit Els Quatre Gats, a bar at Carrer Montsió, 3, which is still open today.

It was here that a young Picasso, who spent his late teens and early twenties in Barcelona, gave his first exhibition. The Museu Picasso on c/ Montcada in Barcelona shows much of his early work, and although the collection includes few of his 'masterpieces', it gives a fascinating insight into the genesis of genius. For an even more profound understanding of the roots of Picasso's creativity, it is also worth visiting Horta de Sant Joan in the Terra Alta comarca in the Province of Tarragona. Picasso spent two extended periods in this small village, and it was here that he almost single-handedly invented Cubism. Picasso is quoted as saying, 'Everything I have learnt, I have learnt at Horta', and the village museum's collection of paintings of Horta's rooftops and people reflect this so incredibly clearly.

Another Catalan artist, who began working in the earlier decades of the 20th century and also maintained the Barcelona-Paris connection, was Joan Miró (1893-1983), whose designs and sculptures are scattered around Barcelona, the city of his birth. He also has a fine museum dedicated to him on Montjuïc. In a similar vein, the wildly eccentric surrealist Salvador Dalí (1904-1989) was born in Figueres, where he inaugurated his equally eccentric museum in 1970.

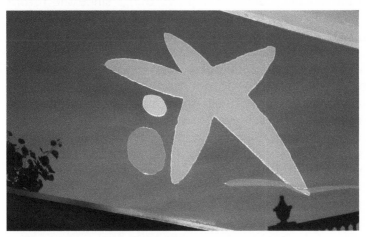

La Caixa - let's face it there's something classy about the Catalans. They even use a design by avantguard artist Joan Miró as the logo for one of their major banks.

Going back to architecture, the 1920s brought in a new style called Noucentisme, whose clean classical lines can be seen on the slopes of Montjuïc as you walk up from Plaça Espanya and in many 20th century government buildings across Catalonia. This was the last truly Catalan architectural movement before the bleak years of Franco's dictatorship. Franco and his henchmen were so hell-bent on destroying Catalonia's heritage that they changed all the names of towns and streets into Castilian, and showed a similar disrespect for the Principality's architectural legacy.

From 1939 to 1975, jerry-built housing and industrial estates sprang up around historic town centres, and it is for this reason that the word *suburbi* in Catalan doesn't mean suburb but is better translated as slum. Romanesque, Gothic and Modernist buildings were allowed to fall into a pitiful state and cynical speculation led to the construction of the eyesores that still line parts of the Catalan coast.

A lot has been done to improve things since the return of democracy. Hoardings have been torn down from historic buildings and facades have been restored. Green spaces have been created in the most depressing areas and the Generalitat has funded an ambitious project to restore statues to their original sites and build modern sculptures when this was impossible. So much has been achieved, but it is true to say that much of the damage done by nearly forty years of fascism is quite simply irreparable. So if you reach the outskirts of one of the town's in the guide, don't be put off by its down at heel appearance – Catalonia still contains beautiful wild green expanses and has many architectural jewels just waiting to be uncovered.

ELS QUATRE GATS

The name of the bar where Picasso, Casas and Rusinyol laid out the blueprint for 20th century painting says a lot about the Catalans' dry sense of humour. If you miss a social event and ask a Catalan who was there, they might well say 'Quatre Gats', literally 'Four Cats', meaning not many people and no-one of any importance. In its heyday, the bar was frequented by some of the most important artists, writers, musicians and radical political figures of the time.

If you go there now, you won't see any Picasso but you will see the bar decorated much as it was a century ago with reproductions of works by Casas and Rusinyol, the group's two leading lights. You can also get a drink and a meal at surprisingly reasonable prices for such an emblematic place.

FOOD AND DRINK

Throughout most of Catalonia you can eat many of the foods that Spain is famous for. Tapas abound but you never get them free in Catalonia (the Catalans, along with the Jews and the Scottish, are famous for being mean – not true actually, but…). You can drink *gazpacho* in summer and eat paellas all year round. However, Catalonia does have its own autochthonous cuisine, and in bars and restaurants you may find a list of weird and wonderful dishes with Catalan names – you won't find a Spanish translation because they are only eaten here, and even monolingual Castilian speakers tend to use the Catalan terms.

The great exception to this rule is Catalonia's culinary flagship *Pa amb Tomaquet*. In Barcelona, everybody eats it all the time, whether the bar is run by Catalans, Andalusians or Galicians you'll generally be asked whether you want *pan con tomate* with your bocadillo. If you say 'Yes', the waiter will take a big squelchy ripe tomato, cut it in half and rub it on the bread. The Catalan word for this is *xucar,* and Catalans will often have long heated discussions about where you can get the best kind of *xucar* tomatoes – generally they agree that it's from a bloke who's got an allotment on the other side of the village. Those who live in Barcelona go up to their home village regularly and bring back tomatoes; they then give them to friends (including me) just to prove their point.

In a slightly better class of eating hole, where the waiter may well address you as 'Sir' or 'Madam' and politely ask if you would like 'Toasted Bread with Tomato', *Pa amb Tomaquet* really comes into its own. Served with cured meats, oily salads of which I'll tell you more later or even better anchovies, this is toasted *Pa de Pagès* rubbed first with garlic in abundance before

39

a liberal dose of tomato pulp is wiped on. *Pa de Pagès* is a light airy bread with a hard crust that when toasted becomes brittle – you bite into it and it kind of explodes in your mouth. It's just crying out to be soaked with virgin olive oil that can generally be found shining greenly in a *cetrill* in the middle of the table. Before the oily crumbs get stuck behind your wisdom teeth, the best policy is to double-whammy with a slice of *fuet* or *xoriço* followed by a glop of something to drink – white wine from the Penedès or Catalan cava would be a fine election but I personally favour a mediana Estrella, a third of a litre of the local beer. And that's just for starters, here's the rest of the menu...

Sopes (Soups)

Escudella – The traditional Christmas soup but now served throughout the year. This creamy vegetable and meat stock is often served with large pieces of chewy pasta floating on top. You might see it listed as *Sopa de Galets*.

Sopa d'all - A garlic soup that can also be quite runny. The Catalans would be appalled but it's great for dipping your *Pa amb Tomaquet* in.

Amanides (Salads)

I've never been particularly impressed by the standard salad that is served with most *Menus del Dia*. Rabbit food is what I call it – too much lettuce and a bit short on onion, tomato and olives. Luckily, there are alternatives.

Amanida Catalana - This is a basic salad with tomatoes, Spanish onion and olives (I like the black ones with the stones still in) but doesn't tend to be quite as heavy on the lettuce as just a simple *amanida*. On top you'll find some cheese and a whole range of *embutits* – *fuet*, *xoriço*, *butifarra blanca* and *negre*. It's worth asking the waiter what each of them is, so you can ask be more specific about the contents of your bocadillo the next time you're feeling a bit peckish – *pa amb tomaquet*, of course.

Escalivada – This is one of my favourites. Aubergines and red peppers are baked in the oven until their skins are black and can easily be peeled off. Once cold, their tender insides are cut into strips and a liberal dose of olive oil is applied – simple but tasty, and also quite aesthetically pleasing.

Esqueixada – A raw salt-cod (*bacallà*) salad with, also raw, peppers, tomatoes, onions and olives covered in a liberal dose of olive oil – great for dipping your bread into and an ideal starter during the sweltering summer months.

Xató – A curious salad that consists of *escarola* (a frilly kind of lettuce) tuna, anchovies and white beans covered in the almondy xató sauce – a worthwhile experience for the more adventurous salad consumer.

In March and April, particularly if you make the trek out of the big city, you'll find restaurants that organise xatonades - kind of weirdo Catalan salad festivals (there are some things I'll never completely understand).

Entrants/Primer Plats (Starters)

Canelons - The Catalan approach to cannelloni has nothing to do with Italian cannelloni apart from the thin strips of pasta that they wrap the stuff in. No tomato sauce here, but rather a creamy béchamel sauce that covers pasta and minced white meat (chicken or turkey are particularly good). They often tend to fall to pieces and turn gooey – who cares as long as they taste good?

Cargols – deliciously chewy snails served in a spicy sauce that trickles down your chin and onto your shirt can come as a starter or as a main course.

Entremesos – We're back on the cured meat or *embutit* again. The best places to eat this are the cheapest bars with dingy Coca Cola signs outside. They'll slap whatever they've got left on your plate - choriço, ham, fuet, butifarra, or chopped, a kind of Catalan spam (pronounced chop'ead) – and then add a few slices of very sweaty cheese. Take a deep draught on your glass of vi negre, Catalan red wine, and enjoy!

Espinacs a la Catalana - An excellent way to get started – spinach with raisins and pine nuts – even better if served with béchamel.

Fabes a la Catalana – This is a relatively dry broad bean stew with lumps of embutit (see above) – just what the doctor ordered on a winter's day when the Tramuntana starts to blow.

Samfaina – A ratatouille-like stew of onions, peppers, aubergine and tomato – ideal with pork chop and chips!

Truita – Unfortunately, the Catalans use the same word for trout and omelette, so you might be in for a surprise. Garlic, mushroom, potato and courgette are the most common omelette fillings, but they are generally seated on top of the bar so order whichever one tickles your fancy.

Arròs (Rice Dishes)

Arròs Negre – This rice is black because it is cooked in squid ink, and is often peppered by unrecognisable antediluvian sea creatures recently dragged up from the depths of the Mediterranean before being chopped up and fried.

If you're planning to eat Arròs Negre it's a good idea to take a toothbrush with you, otherwise you'll look like the Wicked Witch of the North for the rest of the day.

Arròs a la Marinera (Paella) – This is the standard paella with prawns, mussels and clams – speaking personally, this involves too much messing about and wiping your fingers on serviettes.

Paella Valenciana – To be perfectly honest, you get the seafood taste but the gravy's better, and you can eat the lumps of rabbit, chicken or lamb with your knife and fork – much more civilised... and tastier!

Carn (Meat)

Butifarra amb Mongetes – Spicy Catalan sausage served with white beans and lashings of all i oli (garlic mayonnaise).

Conill – Rabbit with chips, samfaina or all i oli – particularly good estofat, in a stew.

Estofat de Vedella – Veal stew

Mandonguilles - Meatballs usually in a thick pea gravy, and if you're really lucky with some lumps of squid thrown in.

Perdius a la Vinagreta – Partridges in a sharp vinegar sauce.

Pernil – Ham if it's cured probably Serrano or Jabugo. The closest thing to English-style ham is Pernil York.

Pollastre – They have loads of ways of cooking chicken – a la planxa (griddled), farcit (stuffed), amb gambas/llagosta (with prawns or lobster), al cava (marinated in Cava).

Peix i Marisc (Fish and Seafood)

Anxoves - You can get anchovies from any old part of the Mediterranean, but the best ones come from L'Escala on the Costa Brava – bring on the garlic, oil and pa amb tomaquet.

Bacallà – It's difficult to get fresh cod here, so Catalan-style salt cod, especially if it comes in a samfaina sauce, is an experience in itself – it's got nothing to do with what you'd get in your local chip shop.

Lluç – The Catalans eat hake in much the same way as we eat cod, but the batter is much finer and lighter – when served with lemon mayonnaise, it doesn't just tickle the taste buds, it explodes them.

Musclos al Vapor – Fresh steamed mussels in a tomato, garlic and onion sauce – the best way to go about eating them is to scrape off the mussels with your teeth and then scoop up a bit of sauce with the empty shell, sucking and chewing as you go – no noise restrictions!

Pop – No not Lucozade, but octopus – the truth is the Galicians are much better at preparing this than the Catalans, so keep your eyes peeled for a Bar Gallego, of which there are many.

Suquet – A delicious mixed fish casserole – once again great for dipping bread in.

Tonyina – Often an enormous lump of tuna in *escabeche* sauce – definitely keep's the wolf from the door!

Truïta – Be careful not to order omelette which is the same word, but Catalan trout is often baked with either a ham stuffing or big slices strewn on top.

Postres (Desserts)

Crema Catalana - A custard-like pudding with a burnt caramel topping – scrumptious – it would be even better if they put bananas in it.

Mel i Mató – If you're suffering from pre-menstrual tension (well, so my wife says, anyway) this is ideal – a dome of curdled cheese covered in copious amounts of honey.

Xurros – Being of a chip shop mentality, this is the one for me. Xurros are a kind of long stringy doughnut cooked for too long in far too much oil. They serve them with a cup of liquid chocolate, which means you'll probably not have to eat again for the rest of the holiday.

Wine

Catalonia Wine Regions   FRANCE

ANDORRA

Figueres **1**

●Girona

3 Manresa

10 Lleida

2 el Masnou

Montsant **8**   **5** Montblanc   **4** Barcelona
Vilafranca del Pendès

9   **7** **6**
Falset   Reus   Tarragona

11
Gandessa

ARAGON

VALENCIA

MEDITERRANEAN

1. Empordá
2. Alella
3. Pla de Bages
4. Penedés
5. Conca de Barberá
6. Tarragona
7. Catalunya
8. Piorat
9. Montsant
10. Costers del Segre
11. Terra Alta

The history of winemaking in Catalonia goes back to 800 BC when the Greeks introduced the vine to the Iberian Peninsula, and Catalan wines were highly esteemed by the Romans. Throughout the Middle Ages, a system known as *rabassa morta* was practised by landowners which permitted tenant farmers to stay on the land until their vines died, and consequently, the pagesos or peasants got very good at keeping their vines alive. During this period, grapes were often taken to the local monastery to be fermented and winemaking began to become an art form.

However, it was not until the late 18th century, when Catalonia was first allowed to trade with the Americas that grape growing became an essential Catalan industry. Rather than producing bulky wine, the vine growers or rabassaires distilled their cheap wines into a fiery brandy called aiguardent, literally burning water, which could be transported to Barcelona and then exported to the Americas much more easily. At the end of the 19th century disaster struck when an aphid called philloxera crossed the border into Catalonia having completely wiped out the French vineyards. Both the French and Catalan wine regions had to be replanted by vines resilient to the parasite, which came principally from California. Many rabassaires were forced off their land and joined the ranks of Barcelona's poor. Their vineyards were taken over by larger landowners and the foundations were laid for mass production. An interesting corollary to this is that most French and Catalan wine comes from vines that were originally American. Being more down to earth, commenting on this is water off a duck's back to the Catalans, but a real stab in the heart to a French wine snob!

At the time of writing, there are currently 11 Catalan DOs (Denominació d'Origen), providing a large selection of table and dessert wines, which range from cheap and cheerful to excellent, and very expensive, vintage wines. Wine production here has come a long way from the Spanish plonk that was manufactured under Franco, but I would still say that if you're after a reasonably priced table wine you're much better off going Spanish than French.

Typically, the Catalans have to be different, so while whites are blanc and rosés are rosat, red wine is called vi negre, which actually means black wine.

Catalonia's best known is wine undoubtedly the Cava DO produced in the Alt Penedès comarca. This sparkling white is produced in exactly the same way as Champagne and derives its name from the underground cellars in which it was originally produced. The basic grape varieties used are macabeu, xarel.lo and parellada, which are fermented to produce a wine base and then, in a process known as *tiratge*, mixed with sugar and yeast before being bottled. During the *tapat* stage, the bottles are sealed hermetically and then for the *criança*, they are laid flat in cellars to ferment for a second time. The wine is later decanted to get rid of any sediment before being corked.

Cava is classified according to the amount of sugar used in the fermentation: Brut (less than 20 grammes per litre), Sec (20-30 grammes per litre), Semisec (30-50 grammes per litre) or Dolç (more than 50 grammes). Brut and Sec, in my opinion, are the most drinkable and go well with any food, whereas as Semisec and Dolç work better as dessert wines. At its best, Cava should be served between 6 and 8°C, and it's worth remembering that, however easily it goes down, it's extremely alcoholic – so before you start on that third bottle, make sure you know how you're going to get home.

If you want to see how cava is produced first hand and get pleasantly tipsy along the way, you should visit Sant Sadurni d'Anoia, the self-styled 'Capital of Cava', which has nearly fifty bubbly-producing bodegas. For a modest admission charge, most give guided tours of the winery finished off by a tasting. The best known are Freixenet (*www.freixenet.es*), right next to the Sant Sadurni railway line about a mile out of town, and Cordoniu (*www.cordoniu.es*) housed in a fine Modernista building by Puig i Cadafalch, where the tour includes a fun train ride through the underground cellars. Although the town itself is not much to write home about, most of the other bodegas also offer tours and information about these can be found on the town's website at *www.santsadurni.org*.

The other big name DO wine of the region is Penedès itself, best known for its fruity whites, which whilst being the only adequate companion for fish are also an excellent tipple on their own – I'm particularly partial to a drop of Blanc Pescador, myself. The region also produces some very well-balanced reds, and the slightly sharp Torres brandy, which is somewhere between the rough and ready brandy produced in the south of Spain and France's connoisseur cognac. A good place to find out about wine production is the comarca's lovely capital Vilafranca del Penedès, which has an excellent wine museum on Plaça Jaume I (*www.vilafranca.com*) and the Torres bodega is also well-worth a visit (*www.torres.es*). For more information about the Penedès DO in general visit *www.dopenedes.es*.

Another wine region worthy of note is El Priorat, which has two DOs, Priorat (*www.priorat.org*) and the relative newcomer, Montsant, both of which produce excellent reds. The slate-filled soil of the comarca means that white grapes aren't really an option, but does give the red a distinctive mineral flavour. Further north, the Empordà-Costa Brava DO, which was formerly better known for its sweet dessert wines such as Garnatxa, is now making some more than acceptable reds. The Alella DO (*www.doalella.com*), just north of Barcelona, has been producing delicious aromatic whites since Roman times, and was chronicled by both Marcial and Pliny. Conca de Barberà (*www.conca.altanet.org*), Costers del Segre, Plà de Bagès, Tarragona and Terra Alta are other regions that also produce some good wines. What's more the clever Catalans have recently created the Catalunya DO, which is a catch-all DO that allows bodegas within the existing Catalan DOs to blend wines with quality control and regulated status, and also draws in nearly 4,000 hectares of scattered vineyards which were formerly unclassified within the DO system.

Wine Links

www.freixenet.es
www.cordoniu.es
www.santsadurni.org
www.vilafranca.com
www.torres.es
www.dopenedes.es
www.priorat.org
www.doalella.com
www.conca.altanet.org

BEER

Whilst producing some great wines, the Catalans also like to guzzle their beer. The main local brew is Estrella, which normally comes in 33cl bottles – just ask for a 'Mitjana Estrella'. If you do drink beer here you'll be partaking in a tradition that goes back much further than wine (vines were only introduced to the Iberian Peninsula by the Greeks in 600BC). Although beer was probably invented in Egypt around 5,000BC, the oldest evidence of beer production in Europe is not in Germany, Belgium or even Britain, but in Catalonia in the Province of Lleida and has been dated to more than 2,000BC. The University of Barcelona even has a department dedicated to the Archaeology of Beer.

TRANSPORT

Airports

Barcelona Airport is situated to the south of Barcelona just outside the town of El Prat and, being close to the C-31 and C-32 main roads, is within easy reach of the city centre. The price of a taxi to Plaça Catalunya should be between €20 and €25 depending on whether you're travelling at the weekend, a holiday or at night and how many bags you've got. There's a bus that goes to and from Plaça Catalunya every 10 minutes or so which costs a modest €3.50 or an even cheaper train that goes every half hour and stops at Sants, Passeig de Gràcia and Estació de França.

If you're going to the Costa Brava or Northern Catalunya, Girona Airport might be a better bet. However, the choice of destinations is much more limited at Girona. The airport is situated about 15km outside the city between the villages of Vilobi d'Onyar and Aiguaviva, and can be easily reached by car if you take the A-7, N-11 or C-25. There is no train service and given that you're likely to be going to Barcelona or the Costa Brava, the cost of a taxi (at over €1 per kilometre plus supplements is likely to be prohibitive). You can either get a taxi to Girona and then take a train or make use of the bus service to some of the most common destinations. The two companies are Sarfa (*www.sarfa.com*) and Sagalés (*www.sagales.com*).

Reus Airport, the third of Catalunya's airports, is located 3km from Reus and 13km from Tarragona on the main T-11 road. There's no train but there are various bus services to Reus (Reus Transport), to Barcelona (Hispano Igualadina) and to the Costa Daurada (Autocares Plana). However, the best option is to get to Reus or Tarragona and then catch the train or bus.

Catalunya's airports are run by AENA (Aeropuertos Españoles y Navigación Aérea) who have an excellent up to date web page in English at *www.aena.es*.

Trains

The national train company Renfe is responsible for running all long and medium distance services in Catalunya. You can check out their webpage at *www.renfe.es*.

However, given their gross inefficiency, the Generalitat is about to take over the administration of train lines in the Barcelona area, so hopefully, by the time you read this, the Rodalies service will be as good as the Barcelona metro or the train-cum-metro Ferrocarrils de la Generalitat (FF.CC), which also serves some of the towns on the edge of Barcelona's industrial belt.

Roads

Catalunya's roads are some of the best in Spain but also some of the most expensive. The tolls on the motorways can be quite hefty so watch out for the letters AP (Autopista de Peatge) when planning your route.

Buses

Most towns provide local bus services – more information will be given in each town guide. For international destinations and trips to other parts of Spain you're likely to have to go through Barcelona's main bus station, l'Estació del Nord. Their web page gives an idea of where you can go and with which company. Visit *www.barcelonanord.com*

Ferries

Ferries from the Balearics dock at the Estació Maritima at the bottom of the Rambles. There is a daily service to Palma, Mallorca and services to Menorca and Ibiza a couple of times a week. You can book your ticket at *www.trasmediterranea.es*

Travel Links

www.sarfa.com
www.sagales.com
www.aena.es
www.renfe.es
www.barcelonanord.com
www.trasmediterranea.es

CLIMATE

It's hard to provide an overview of the climate here, as it changes so radically depending where you are. Although the weather is significantly better in Catalonia than in Carlisle, if you live here all year round the cliché of 'Sunny Spain' is a little simplistic.

I personally hate the summer months in Barcelona because it's one thing to be sitting on a beach terrace sipping a beer and quite another having to work in the hot humid heat. You get to work by metro in an atmosphere of suffocation and BO and then have to spend the rest of the day sweating profusely because the air conditioning is never up to the job. In spring and autumn, you might also get caught in a rainstorm; these incredible downpours can last for anything from five minutes to a week and are nothing like anything that you ever experience in Britain; the skies just open, there's no escape and you end up soaked to the skin and searching for the paracetamol to offset the on-coming cold. Inland, particularly around the plains of Vic, there is a mid-winter fog that has much more to do with mushy peas than pea soup; I got stuck in one once and really couldn't see more than a foot in front of me.

Up north on the Costa Brava, a wind, called the Tramuntana, blows for days on end. The people get nervous and depressed and it has been suggested that this is why the region has produced so many great surrealist artists (they're mad!)

However, there's something about living here that I now realise I could never live without, and that's the light. I've just come in to write this from the balcony of the flat; the sun was shining; the day was bright; I heard ripples of laughter coming from the patios below. And what does October mean back in Britain? Grey days, grey days and more grey days. The weather here might not be all it's cracked up to be, but I know that if brutal weather hits us, it'll be over in a flash. We'll be able to breathe again. We'll be able to smile again. I wouldn't change it for the world.

Barcelona Province

The inland, pre-Pyrenean comarcas of Berguedà and Osona have the lowest temperatures in winter and can go down to -10°C or less. The highest temperatures in the high 30s or sometimes low 40s are found in the inland comarcas of l'Alt Penedès, l'Anoia, el Vallès Occidental and el Vallès Oriental usually in July and August.

Girona Province

As you'd expect the comarcas with the lowest temperatures, regularly -15°C or lower are the Pyrenean comarcas of Cerdanya and Ripollès. The highest in the high 30s or sometimes low 40s are usually in la Selva comarca, closer to the Costa Brava.

Lleida Province

Due to the huge differences in geography, extremes are found here all year round. In the Pyrenean comarcas of Pallars Sobirà and Val d'Aran temperatures of up to -20°C are common in winter and there are frosts even in the height of summer. It gets almost as cold in l'Alt Urgell and Solsonès. Lower land in the south reaches the highest summer temperatures with high 30s or sometimes low 40s.

Tarragona Province

The southernmost of the Catalan provinces, Tarragona generally has the mildest winter temperatures though it can still reach -8°C or lower in inland comarcas like la Conca de Barberà and Priorat. Summer highs in the upper 30s or sometimes low 40s are common in Conca de Barberà, Priorat and Ribera d'Ebre.

Catalonia Temperature and Rainfall

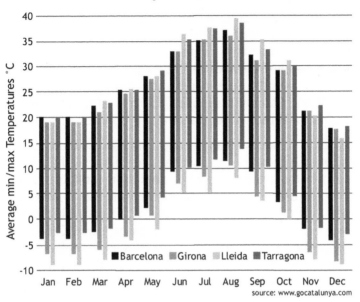

source: www.gocatalunya.com

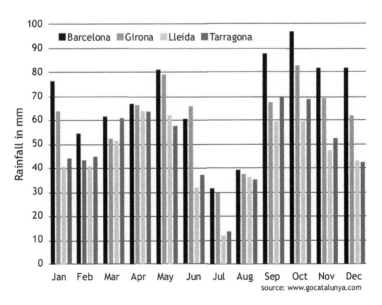

source: www.gocatalunya.com

ECONOMY

With its strong commercial and manufacturing base, Catalonia has long been Spain's most vibrant and competitive economic region, and ranks number 11 in Europe. Despite the fact that it covers less than 7% of the country's surface area and has around 15% of the population, Catalonia supplies approximately 20% of the gross national product and a similar proportion of exports.

Although it lacks energy and mineral resources, its economy relies on industrial companies that have traditionally attracted immigrants from Andalusia, and currently are drawing on workers from Latin America, North Africa and Eastern Europe. Industrial wealth, however, is not evenly spread throughout Catalonia; 85% of companies are concentrated around Barcelona while the petrochemical industry is centred in Tarragona and the timber and cork trades in Girona.

The distribution of Catalonia's working population follows the same pattern as in most other developed countries, with 7% involved in farming, 49% in manufacturing and 44% in the services sector. The latter accounts for more than half of Catalonia's gross domestic product, followed by industry, and to a lesser degree, building, farming and fishing. At around 12%, the rate of unemployment is relatively low compared to the rest of Spain.

If iron and steel production has traditionally been the prerogative of Asturias and the Basque Country, the metal-working industry, a thriving sector which benefits from foreign investment and covers light engineering and the manufacture of transport equipment, is firmly Catalan. The automobile industry is also important in Catalonia, accounting until recently for a large proportion of the production of SEAT, the Spanish car manufacturing company.

Catalonia is also ahead of the Basque Country in rubber processing and plastics, and leads Madrid in the chemical industry, which manufactures products used in agriculture, industry and pharmaceuticals. Similarly, the computer sector is developing fast and Catalonia, through its involvement in European science and technology research programs, runs a close second to Madrid in the manufacture of electronics equipment such as components and integrated circuits.

While the chemical, metallurgical, food, leather and shoe industries are expanding, the textile industry, which dates back to the Middle Ages, is showing a noticeable drop in production. Even so, Catalonia still leads Spain in the textile and clothing industries, employing more workers in spinning and weaving than any other region.

The present boom in the tertiary sector, mainly banking, tourism, and trade, came about after the death of Franco in 1975, and the 1992 Olympic Games reinforced this healthy area of the Catalan economy. This sector is further boosted by a massive domestic and foreign tourism trade that numbers about 15 million people a year and is mainly centred on the Costa Brava and Costa Daurada and their hinterland, although skiing and rural and cultural tourism are increasingly strong. In turn, tourism ensures the development of the region's roads, hotels, golf courses, marinas, thermal spas and so on. Similarly, most foreign banks have offices in Catalonia alongside the region's own very healthy banking sector, which ranks fifth on the European scale.

Agriculture, now highly mechanised, accounts for only 3% of Catalonia's income, although Catalonia is still one of Spain's main farming regions, but wonderful Catalan produce tends to stay here to be consumed by the locals. While the wetter mountainous northern part of Catalonia grows mainly fodder crops and concentrates on stock-raising, the coastal regions, particularly in the south, tend to be more diversified with vineyards, olives, almonds and market gardening.

Given such a diverse economy and so many international companies, there are many work opportunities for foreigners in Catalonia, which might be why you're reading this Going Native Guide in the first place. If your own company is sending you they'll probably do all the sorting out from your end, but just in case the address of the Spanish Embassy in Britain is at 39 Chesham Place, London, SW1X 8SB, Tel. +44 20 72355555 (http://spain.embassyhomepage.com) and the British Consulate in Barcelona is Avinguda Diagonal 477 Tel. 93 366 6200 (*www.ukinspain.com*).

If you just turn up here, decide you like it and need to do some work to fund a semi-sabbatical, then there's always bar and restaurant work in the tourist belt. The major cities and the costas tend to have large ex-pat communities so there are always opportunities for English-speaking self-employed plumbers, electricians and builders. I've also seen adverts for English-speaking doctors, dentists, physiotherapists and lawyers, but many people come to Catalonia to teach English as a foreign language (see below).

If you intend to work in Catalonia, just like in the rest of Spain, you will need to get your papers in order. For EU citizens the process begins with registering as a resident with your local Ajuntament, a process known as 'empadronar-se'. Having done this, you will then need to obtain a NIE, Numero de Identidad Extranjero or Foreign Identity Number, which also serves as tax number. Given the level of bureaucracy this is a laborious process and you will have to go a number of times because you are bound to have forgotten a crucial document. Your local Ajuntament or police station should be able to give you the address of the nearest office.

English Language Teaching (ELT)

Twenty years ago you could turn up in Barcelona and being English was the only qualification you needed to get a job teaching English, but things have moved on since then. Nowadays a CELTA (Certificate of English Language Teaching to Adults) is a minimum requirement, and some experience or a PGCE is definitely an advantage.

The CELTA can be studied over an extended period or as a month-long full-time course and will give you the basics on how to teach English using the Communicative Approach, which to simplify things a little values communicative ability over accuracy and concentrates on learning by doing. An underlying tenet of the approach is 'If you tell me, I hear. If you explain to me, I understand. If you involve me, I learn.'

There are many places in Britain where you can study for this Cambridge University-backed qualification (there's also a Trinity College equivalent, by the way), and an increasing number of centres across Catalonia. Perhaps the best-known, certainly amongst my generation is International House in Barcelona (International House, c/ Trafalgar 14 Tel. 93 268 4511 *www.ihes.com*). Before you sign up for the course, it's well-worth reading Jeremy Harmer's classic 'The Practice of English Language Teaching', which will give you an overview of the basic methodological approach, and as most English speakers don't actually know very much about their own language, a grammar reference book is indispensable. My favourite is Michael Swan's 'Practical English Usage', and although your tutors will

59

probably tell you never to use it in class, Raymond Murphy's 'English Language in Use' will get you out of a lot of sticky situations, particularly as you take your first steps in teaching. It's actually designed for students with a grammar explanation on one page and some exercises on the opposite page, but if you get asked to teach the Third Conditional or Passives, for example, you can read up on it, do the exercises and you'll be in a much better position to answer the niggly questions that students tend to ask.

The best time to look for work is September as the ELT academic begins in the first week of October. This will involve getting your CV around to as many schools as possible, and if you're in Barcelona make sure you buy La Vanguardia newspaper on Sunday because it has an excellent classified ads section at the back. You can also try offering private classes, but in order to make it worth your while you need to charge €25-30 an hour, which is quite a lot for an individual, so you really need to set up groups of students. You might find a company willing to take you on, or if you live out in the sticks where there are no language schools, you could set up a classroom at home, and advertise locally.

FESTAS

If there's one thing that you can say about the Catalans is that they love to party. Every town has its own Festa Major, when people parade through the streets, organise concerts, drink and eat and generally have a wonderful time. The festivals are family-oriented by day and more hedonistic by night, but as everybody likes to have fun, almost any public holiday can become an excuse for something much more elaborate.

Street parades are the centrepiece of many festivals, and often include floats on the back of lorries or a line of typical characters on foot. Every parade will have *gegants*, which are large figures of about three metres high with a person inside, *capgrossos*, quite literally fatheads, and *trabucaires*, groups of men who shoot 18th century blunderbusses into the air making a lot of noise and leaving a strong smell of gunpowder. *Diables* dress up as drum-playing devils by day and run through the streets with fireworks in their hands at night for the *correfoc*, the running fire.

Correfocs are held all over Catalonia. If you don't want to get 'sulphured out' as they run through the streets be sure to wear a scarf and carry a bottle of water. If you get there before the fire run, you'll also have the privilege of hearing some of the most transcendental drumming in Christendom.

People who like getting involved in processions seem to take it up as a full-time hobby, so any small-town Festa Major will be visited by groups from other towns making it much more spectacular than the town's population might lead you to believe. There will also be *sardanas*, the traditional Catalan circle dance, accompanied by a *cobla*, or small orchestra, in the evening, and if you're really lucky a *concurs de castellers* might be organised.

These are competitions in which *casteller* groups build human castles that rise to a height of ten metres and are breathtakingly spectacular.

Below is a list of the public holidays and festivals celebrated across the whole of Catalonia. In the town guides, I have included more specific information about the must-see events in each location. If you want to know what's going on near you at any time of the year, visit *www.festes.org*, which lists all the festivals for the coming month. Although it's in Catalan, you'll get the places and dates, and you're sure to have a great time.

A team of brave castellers working together in Barcelona.

Jan 1st – New Year's Day is a much-needed public holiday after the festivities of the night before. New Year's Eve is generally spent among family and friends, and bars and restaurants often close at 10pm and open again at 1am, when everybody hits the streets again to celebrate the New Year. If you get invited to someone's home, you'll be expected to *'menjar el raïm'*, eat the grapes, along with everyone else. This consists of eating a grape on each chime of the bells at 12 o'clock, which is much more difficult than it sounds. Your mouth ends up full of pips and skin, which you have to wash down with a glass of cava. The singing and drunkenness doesn't start until much later.

Jan 6th – On the evening of the fifth, the Three Kings, Els Reis, arrive and there is an amazing procession through most towns with gegants, capgrossos and diables and fantastically decorated floats sponsored by local companies and community groups. The stars of the show, though, are the Kings themselves, Gaspar, Melcior, and Baltasar, who are paraded through the streets on massive thrones. Everybody throws sweets to the children assembled at the side of the street, so be sure to take a plastic bag and be prepared to scramble for them. For the following day, Festa de Reis itself, children leave shoes out on the balcony or in the backyard overnight, and wake up to find them full of presents.

Carnaval or Carnestoltes – This is the holiday we know as Shrove Tuesday, but here it's the last moment of debauchery before fasting and religious obedience during Lent. It generally involves a lot of partying as semi-clad ladies parade through the streets. While in Sitges, Catalonia's most famous parade, you get to feast your eyes on extraordinarily convincing and provocative transvestites. It's also a time to eat *bunyols*, which are kind of misshapen aniseed-flavoured doughnut. In comparison, our Pancake Day is a load of crepes.

Gegants - during the Festa Major these giants are paraded through the streets.

Setmana Santa or Pasqua – Good Friday and Easter Monday are both public holidays, but beginning a week earlier on Palm Sunday, when children walk through the street carrying gigantic dried palm leaves, the whole week is an excuse for processions and religious music. Although Easter Sunday is quite a solemn affair, when tortured effigies of Christ are paraded through the streets, Easter in Catalonia does contain some lighter moments. Children traditionally receive a *mona* from their godparent in the morning. This is a large ornate chocolate model that makes the average British Easter egg look a little pathetic. Also be sure not to miss *l'ou com balla,* the dancing egg, which is an egg that is balanced on the fountain in the centre of the cloister of the local cathedral dancing its symbolic dance throughout the whole of Easter week.

April 23rd – El Dia de Sant Jordi, Saint George's Day, is also known as the Day of the Book and the Rose. Sant Jordi has been the patron saint of Catalonia since medieval times, and although his dragon-slaying legend is much the same as the English version, his feast day is something quite special here. The streets are full of people selling roses and stalls piled high with books, which men buy for women and women buy for men respectively. As both Shakespeare and Cervantes died on April 23rd, the medieval poetry festival, the *Jocs Florals* was moved to this day, so everybody from schoolchildren to professional poets writes a special celebratory verse. Aware that the Catalans were setting an example for the world, UNESCO declared April 23rd International Day of the Book in 1995.

The 'Four Fingers of Blood' of the Catalan flag and the red rose, the symbol of love and romance, are everywhere to be seen on Sant Jordi's day.

May 1st – Labour Day is a public holiday often accompanied Trades Union processions.

June 23ʳᵈ – La Verbena de Sant Joan, Midsummer's Eve, is Catalonia's craziest festival. There are firework displays, correfocs and street parties all over the Principality. Be prepared to drink enormous quantities of cava and have breakfast before you go to bed.

August 15th – L'Assumpció a religious public holiday.

September 11th – La Diada, Catalonia's National Day, is celebrated to remember the day that after a long siege Barcelona fell to the Castilian troops and Catalonia lost all its legal, political, linguistic and cultural rights. Normally, La Senyera, the Catalan Flag, is flown from balconies all over the Principality. Throughout years of repression under Franco and more recently, when Aznar was president of Spain, multitudinous demonstrations were organised. However, given Zapatero's positive attitude towards the Catalans, since the Socialist government came to power in 2004, the day has been strangely quiet. As there's nothing to demonstrate about, celebrations are limited to laying a wreath at the statue of Rafael Casanovas, the hero of the siege of Barcelona.

October 12th – La Festa de la Hispanitat, the Festival of Spanishness, is just an excuse to have a day off work.

November 1st – Tots Sants, All Saints' Day, is traditionally when people visit cemeteries to remember their deceased loved ones. It also coincides with the Castanyada when roast chestnuts are eaten. For those with a sweet tooth, panallets are a must at this time of the year. These small marzipan balls come in a variety of flavours – my favourites are the coconut-flavoured ones or the ones covered in pine nuts.

December 6th – Dia de la Constitució, the Day of the Constitution, is a public holiday remembering the day when Spain's democratic constitution was drawn up after the death of Franco.

December 8th – La Immaculada is another religious public holiday. Most people take advantage of the 'pont' or bridge idea, which reasons that when there is only one day between two day's off work, whether they be a weekend or a public holiday, it's not worth going to work. On a good year when the 6th is a Tuesday and the 8th is a Thursday, you get a wonderful week's holiday, which means you can get all your shopping done just in time for Christmas.

Christmas – Nadal, Christmas Day, and Sant Esteve, Boxing Day, are both public holidays, but Christmas is quite a low-key affair, generally celebrated with the family. Most towns put on Nativity Plays or erect Nativity Scenes, sometimes with live figures. Keep an eye out for, El Caganer, who crouches at the back of the stable doing what most of us do in the private of our own toilet. The traditional Caganer is a figurine wearing Catalan national dress with the products of his bowel movements graphically located underneath his bottom, but Caganers are also collectors' items and often depict famous people. He is generally regarded as a peasant symbol fertilising the earth but perhaps he's just eaten too much *turró*, the delicious almond-flavoured sweet, so typical of the Christmas period.

If there's one thing that you can say about the Catalans is that they love to party.

GOING NATIVE IN CATALONIA

Many books have been written to help people who are moving to or have recently arrived in Spain – Yolanda Solo's *'Spain: The Expat Survival Guide'* also published by NativeSpain is a good example, by the way. These books provide the reader with excellent information on settling into a new culture, things you should bear in mind, possible problems, legal advice and weblinks so you can source the material yourself.

The aims of this book, however, are a little different. Firstly, we are 'Going Native in Catalonia', and if you've read this far, I'm sure you'll be aware that tips on Spain are not always applicable to Catalonia. So if you're serious about coming here, I suggest you do research, read widely and use the web addresses mentioned in this book as starting points for your investigations. Secondly, as I've been living here for so long, I no longer remember the problems I had when I came here, and to be perfectly honest the Catalan way of doing things now seems much more obvious to me than any other.

Twenty years, though, do count for something, because in that time I've seen a lot of people come and go. Some seemed to be doomed to fail right from the start. Others were obviously just passing through; they came for a limited period, enjoyed their time here and then decided to get on with 'serious living' back in their country of origin. And yet another group, to which I belong myself, decided for whatever reason to stay and stay and stay. People like me are no longer expats, we really have 'Gone Native', and not surprisingly we're quite a homogeneous bunch.

What do successful long-term residents have in common?

- They are adaptable and tolerant. This means that the initial culture shock and different way of doing things can be taken on with ease.

- They're individualistic and independent. Not hanging out with people who are the same as you allows you to make your own way in a new culture. You need to be able to enjoy difference and diversity whilst retaining a strong sense of your own identity.

- They're good language learners. If you haven't already got at least an 'A' level in French or Spanish, you will need to apply yourself to learning Catalonia's two official languages with commitment and enthusiasm. The only way to get anywhere in Catalonia is to learn Catalan and Spanish as quickly and effectively as possible.

- They're thick-skinned but open-minded. Foreign tourists get ripped off and occasionally insulted in every country in the world. Bad experiences should be water off a duck's back, so don't trick yourself into believing that everybody shares the opinions of the occasional racist.

- Their plans are flexible. Amongst the successful long-term residents I know the reasons for coming here in the first place are extremely diverse; a post-MA exchange programme, to practise the language after completing a Spanish degree, to become a professional flamenco dancer or, in my case, because I was offered a free place to stay for a few months. If asked, most of us will tell you that we stayed because we liked it, life events seemed to be telling us that this was the place to be, and that if we'd had any regrets we would have moved on.

- They've got emotional ties here. Whether these be friends, partners or children, after a while it's important to have the people you love most close to you. There are people I miss back home but it's impossible for me to see my wife and daughter as foreigners.

- They maximise their skills in two directions. Whether you're an engineer, a dentist or a rock musician, the knowledge you bring with you is an important selling point. Once you've learned how things work here you have insider information that is saleable back home. A simple example is teaching English language and culture to the Catalans and then writing about Catalonia for the English-speaking market!

- They 'Think Positive'. However long you stay, there'll be good days and bad days. The trick is to focus on what you like about being here. In my case, this is the light; so being able to have breakfast in bright (but cold) sunshine on my terrace in mid-January is a great cure for any ills.

Not everybody wants to spend the rest of their life away from their home country. A short stay of a few months to a couple of years can be fulfilling and rewarding and will be an experience that will stay with you forever. However, there are certain people that from day one seem doomed to fail – you can normally spot them a mile away and I suggest you avoid them like the plague.

- People who are continually criticising life back home. They arrive rubbishing everything they've left behind. Within a few months they'll be rubbishing the life they've built around themselves.

- People who are running away from something. Some shady characters go to live in far-flung lands, but a more common example is couples who think a change of air might sort things out between them. Often it just exacerbates underlying problems and brings them out into the open.

- People who assume everything's going to be the same as it was back home. You're going to have to adapt to a new lifestyle. You're going to have to learn a new language. Most of your assumptions about how things should be done are going to be challenged. If you're not prepared to take this on board, you're better off staying at home.

- People who are constantly homesick. I also miss so many tangible and intangible things, but if things were so great back home, why did you leave in the first place?

- People with no money. Not only are they irritating sponges who don't bother to find a local source of income before it's too late, but they'll be running back home soon (probably owing you a few Euros!)

Not everybody wants to spend the rest of their life away from their home country. A short stay of a few months to a couple of years can be fulfilling and rewarding and will be an experience that will stay with you forever.

So what is the key to making a successful move?

This obviously depends on your age and the degree to which you wish to integrate, but know this before you go, and get some experience before you burn your boats.

Younger people (18-40)

If you are young(ish) and still in a position to decide where your life wants to go, there are a number of options open to you.

- Undergraduates. Recent changes in the European education system have given Catalan universities parity with other European higher education institutions. The ERASMUS programme (www.erasmus.ac.uk), which has operated since 1987, gives students the chance to spend 3 to 12 months in a foreign country continuing their education and gaining all-important credits. Exchanges are usually organised by the home university, so everything is set up before you leave. Language, though, is an important consideration. There are plans to introduce a quota of 10% of lectures in English but at the moment the majority of study is done in Catalan and to a lesser extent Castilian. The main Catalan universities have modern language services where you can learn the local languages and gain credits at the same time. The main receptor of ERASMUS students is the Universitat Autònoma de Barcelona (*www.uab.cat*) but it's also worth googling Universitat Rovira i Virgili, Universitat de Barcelona and Universitat Pompeu Fabra for up-to-date info.

- Postgraduates. Don't underestimate the broad range of courses on offer for Master's degrees and the excellent level of tutoring for doctoral theses. You would be mad to even think about it without a competent level of Spanish; working Catalan can be learnt once you get here.

- English Teaching. Long gone are the days when you could turn up and get a job just because you spoke English. You will need a CELTA (the basic teaching certificate available through Cambridge TESOL) or the Trinity equivalent, which can be obtained in the UK and, once qualified, you'll be able to apply for jobs in the educational supplements of the British broadsheets. Another option would be to take a one-month intensive course in Barcelona at International House (www.ihes.com) or one of the many other Teacher Training schools. This would be a good way to test the water and, as the course organisers are in touch with local schools, you might end up being offered a job.

- A Proper Job. If you work for an international company with offices in Catalonia, you could join the increasing number of workers who take advantage of a secondment abroad. Your company's Human Resources department should be able to organise everything for you. Similarly, pages such as www.jobsinbarcelona.es provide contact info for job opportunities for professional people. Bear in mind, though, that a move might also involve a drop in salary.

Accommodation is obviously going to be an issue. Agencies like *www.desigbarcelona.com* cater for the top end of the market, but if you're looking for something cheaper and are prepared to share, you're best looking at the bulletin boards at the universities, escoles oficials and language schools.

Older People (35-70+)

Whilst many people will always come to Catalonia to spend their retirement, this group has been joined by an increasing number of young professionals, who often as a result of the Internet are able to continue their career in sunnier climes. If you belong to one of these groups, you will have an independent income. But even so making Catalonia your permanent home requires a great deal of thought, planning and research.

Going Native Links

www.erasmus.ac.uk
www.uab.cat
www.jobsinbarcelona.es
www.desigbarcelona.com

A Research Visit

If, during your wild and reckless youth, you did some travelling and these travels brought you to Catalonia for a period of time, then you'll know the score (things have changed superficially in the last 20 years, but the essence of everything remains the same). However, if you fell in love with the place whilst here on holiday, you would be foolish not to get an idea of what it's like to live here all year round.

You could plan a number of short trips at different times of the year, but if I were you I'd commit myself to something a little longer. A visit that would give you time to learn about, reflect on and possibly prepare a future permanent move – a short section in a book like this cannot do that for you.

This should be done out of season, as particularly on the coast and the more touristy areas, renting will be a lot cheaper. You'll have the chance to see what life is like when all the crowds have gone away. Your favourite restaurant may be closed. British newspapers won't be on sale. You may have to get in the car just to do your basic shopping. Furthermore, you'll find that nobody speaks English anymore so, if you still like it, this may be the time to take that language course that you'd always meant to take but never got round to.

Where are you going to live?

- Barcelona. Remember that a weekend break in the Catalan capital and living here permanently are two different things entirely. You will never be short of entertainment, culture and a cosmopolitan atmosphere, but don't expect to leave the rat race behind you. Furthermore, gone are the days when you could pick up a flat at a snip, and house prices now are on a par with any other capital city (if not higher!) Although the ability to speak Catalan would certainly open doors for you, you are probably best prioritising your Castilian as the city is completely bilingual.

- Provincial Capitals and Small Towns. A more laid-back option which will bring you closer to the authentic Catalan experience. Property bargains can still be found. Depending where you go, you might get by with only Castilian but in many towns (particularly inland) you'll find yourself a little cut-off unless you learn Catalan.

- Villages and Rural Isolation. If you go inland, you can still find reasonably priced properties in idyllic settings, but these will often require quite a lot of work. You have to be clear how much you can do yourself and how much you're prepared to pay to have the house of your dreams. You should also remember that rural isolation can be very, well, *isolated* and even the most basic facilities will probably be a drive away. This may be just what you want when you're young and fit but might become more of a problem, as you get increasingly dependent on health care, for example.

- Urbanitzacions. These housing estates normally provide individual houses built on a plot of land. Often situated within easy reach of the coast, they are home to a mix of Catalans, Spanish and foreigners, who may live there permanently or use them as holiday homes. Prices vary depending on the size of the property and the number of communal facilities, and you may see homes advertised 'off the peg' (you buy the property before it has been built). There are a number of risks involved in the latter option, as you often don't know exactly when the urbanització will be finished, what it will look like when it is or what the community atmosphere will be like. The nature of the community is important as you will probably be obliged to join the Communitat de Proprietaris, a house owners group that administers costs and projects that are common to the community. These projects may be quite mundane but it is not unheard of that they include the building of a swimming pool, the roads and the installation of telephone lines or even electricity, so I suggest that you (and your lawyer) do an adequate amount of research before you commit yourself.

- Costa Communities. Sections of both the Costa Brava and the Costa Daurada are home to sprawling housing developments of row after row of holiday homes. If you intend to occupy your property all year round prices can be very reasonable. However, you should be aware that many are quite limited in their facilities as they are designed to be lived in during the summer months – roughing it for a couple of weeks is one thing, but limitations (heating, space) might become all too apparent when cold winter winds begin to blow. Furthermore, out of season that delightfully bustling summer town might become completely deserted, and when there are no customers all the shops, bars and restaurants will close down too.

A Final Thought

My own experience of living in Catalonia means that I can heartily recommend it as a place to live and be, but I can only give you sketchy guidelines on how you can make life here work for you. I would say, though, that above all you should get yourself good independent legal advice and make sure you look before you leap!

Bona sort!

Town and City Guide

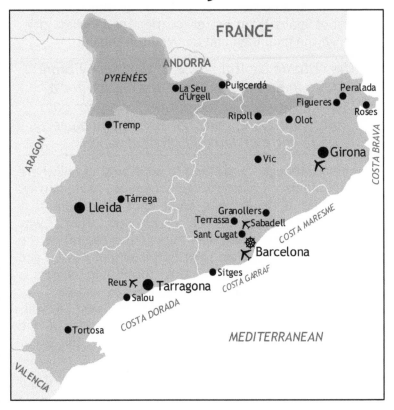

BARCELONA

Population: 1,593,075

It is impossible to think of Catalonia without Barcelona dominating your thoughts. But if it's impossible to conceive of Catalonia without its capital, it's impossible to sense Barcelona without its barris and districts; the places where we live; the nuts and bolts of the coolest city in Europe. The place is a consequence of its geography and its people. It's a happy mix, a

79

pluricultural hotchpotch, and always has been. This city can tolerate immigration because it can absorb new ideas – it's absorbed me, anyway! It should be the capital of Spain. What better location for a kickass city – between the mountain and the Mediterranean?

> *The Catalan capital is one of the most vibrant cities in Europe; an ideal destination for a weekend break, a hot option for a year out after university, and not such a bad place to get married and settle down in.*

Barcelona, though, is too wild to be capital of anywhere but Catalonia. Centralist governments have always known that ports bring a confluence of people that might be a danger to the status quo. That's why Washington rather than New York is the capital of the USA, Moscow rather than Saint Petersburg of Russia, and the fact that Brasilia rather than the Rio de Janeiro is the capital of Brazil never ceases to amaze. No, Barcelona will never be the capital of Spain. It will, however, insist on being itself – the Shadow of the Wind, the City of Marvels, the Rose of Fire, the Great Enchantress. BARCELONA – pure and simple.

If you get enchanted by the Great Enchantress, you'll need to sort yourself out. In order to get anything done in other towns, you'll need to go to your local Ajuntament.

But the Ajuntament de Barcelona is a bit too mega to deal with the average citizen, so each district has an Oficina d'Atenció al Ciutadà – you'll know you're in the right place when you see OAC in big red letters on the door. They are open from 8.30 till 5.30 in the winter but close at 2.15 from July to September. When not mentioned the contact number is 900 226 226 or 010.

Ajuntament de Barcelona, Plaça Sant Jaume, 1 Tel. 93 402 7000 *www.bcn.cat*

CIUTAT VELLA

Population: 113,154

The Ciutat Vella, Barcelona's old town, is still its centre and, for most people, the start of any visit to the city, however long or short. In reality, it comprises the four ancient barris of the Barri Gòtic and La Ribera, both to the left of Les Rambles as you walk down from Plaça Catalunya, El Raval, to the right, and La Barceloneta, which veers off to the left once you reach the Columbus statue at the bottom.

If you're looking for a place to stay, a good place to find a reasonably-priced hostal is on the left of Les Rambles before you get to the Liceu metro station.

Les Rambles itself is actually five streets in one; Rambla de Canaletes, d'Estudis, de Sant Josep, de Caputxins and de Santa Mònica. Recent tourist propaganda makes the improbable claim that there's now a sixth, the Rambla del Mar, but although delightful, it's best to take that with a pinch of salt. You could spend a whole day on Les Rambles and, like Lorca, still end up wishing it would never end, because it's not just a spectacle put on for tourists but a living, breathing event created and used by the *Barcelonins* themselves. They sell flowers and animals, make music and mime and further down even prostitute themselves. A walk down Les Rambles is to Barcelona what a journey to the centre of the Earth is to the planet we inhabit, and it's a street that everyone in Barcelona comes back to again and again.

If you're looking for a place to stay, a good place to find a reasonably-priced hostal is on the left of Les Rambles before you get to the Liceu metro station. This area, unlike El Raval and the Rambles below Plaça Reial, retains the feel of medieval Barcelona but is also safe at night. This means that you can enjoy the twisted streets of the Ciutat Vella by day and its wild nightlife by night without ever having to get on the metro.

The Barri Gòtic, which is reached from the Rambles by walking down Carrer Ferran just by Metro Liceu, is the oldest part of the old town, the best-preserved Gothic city centre in Europe with its origins dating back even further to Roman times. Its heart is Plaça Sant Jaume, which houses the Generalitat and the Ajuntament, and so is the administrative and political centre of both Barcelona and Catalonia. The only way to discover the Barri Gòtic is to explore its backstreets; the Cathedral, Plaça del Rei, Plaça del Pi, to name just a few of the barri's jewels, quite simply throb with history and cultural interest. If you walk down Carrer Ciutat next to the Ajuntament building, you'll find lots of old working-class bodegas, where you can eat tapas with the locals, and after filling your stomach I'd recommend dancing the night away at Karma or Jamboree on Plaça Reial.

Having crossed Plaça Sant Jaume, you will reach Via Laietana, which marks the border between the Barri Gòtic and La Ribera district on the other side. The most important monuments here are the sumptuous Santa Maria del Mar, possibly the finest example of Gothic architecture, 15th century Carrer Montcada, where you'll find the Picasso Museum, and further up the hill, in what is technically the barri of Sant Pere Lluís, Domènech i Montaner's modernist gem – the Palau de la Música Catalana. Tired of tramping the streets, you can rest your weary feet in the Parc de la Ciutadella, originally the site of a citadel built by the Castilians to subjugate the people of Barcelona and transformed into a park for the 1888 International Exhibition. The park also contains Barcelona Zoo and the seat of the Catalan Parliament, and is just five minutes from El Born, one the city's hippest places to eat and drink.

From El Born make your way down the slight hill to the port and on your left you'll find the working-class barri of La Barceloneta, originally developed in the mid 18th century to house the people displaced by the building of the citadel 50 years earlier. As you approach Barceloneta along Passeig de Borbó, which gives on to the luxury marina and is lined with swish seafood eateries, the barri looks upmarket. However, behind the façade, it's still the rough and ready Barceloneta of old with rundown bars and squares where children play and drunks sleep off their last session. Some, though, make their way to the other side of the barri, to the blue flag beaches of Barceloneta and Sant Sebastià, which were cleaned up in time for Barcelona's 1992 Olympics and are now amongst the finest city beaches on the Mediterranean coast.

Doubling back through Barceloneta to the marina, a walk along the harbour will take you back to the Columbus monument from where you can explore the other side of the Rambles, El Raval. Apart from the wonderful Maritime Museum, this part of town is pretty rundown and you may well be accosted by a prostitute of indeterminable age and gender. Centuries ago this area was once open fields where produce was grown to feed a hungry and overpopulated city, but its proximity to the port meant that it gradually turned into a red-light district known as the Barrio Chino. It was here in the 1930s that Jean Genet lived the marginal existence of a rent-boy that he recounts in The Thief's Journal. Although much improved, El Raval retains much of its razzamatazz, and is home to great drinking haunts such as Bar Marsella or London Bar where the smell of absinthe, now illegal, still permeates the atmosphere, and for the really raunchily-inclined the live sex shows at Baghdad are a must.

As you move up the Rambles, El Raval loses some of its exhilarating sense of danger and gains in culture with Gaudí's Palau Güell and Catalonia's operatic shrine, El Liceu. Its climax, though, is the weird and wonderful Boqueria market, which harks back to the barri's time as Barcelona's market garden, and is the place to take in the invigorating aromas of fruit and fish after smelling the seedier side of the city.

Oficina d'Atenció al Ciutadà, Carrer Ramelleres, 17 Tel. 900 226 226

The Boqueria market on the Rambles is one of the must-go-there places in Barcelona - the smells, the sounds, a market atmosphere that is impossible to find anywhere else.

LES RAMLBES

In most conventional guidebooks, the Catalan word 'Rambles' is written as 'Ramblas', the Castilian spelling. I suppose this makes a reasonable amount of sense as in both Catalan and Castilian, the singular is 'Rambla', and in Castilian just as in English plurals are formed by adding an 's' to a singular noun. Catalan plurals, however, change the 'a' of the singular to the 'e' and then add an 's' in order to retain the same pronunciation.

So the words are spelt differently but pronounced in the same way, and as Les Rambles (pronounced Ramblas) is the most famous street in Barcelona the capital of Catalonia, it makes more sense to me to write it in Catalan. Furthermore, I just like the word because it looks like the third person singular of the English verb 'to ramble' as in 'He rambles down Les Rambles', which, of course, is what everybody does.

Tourist Offices (Oficines de Turisme)

Plaça Catalunya, 17 (Tel.93 285 38 34) is the main tourist office giving the most complete information service, including restaurant and accommodation booking, and really should be the first stop on any visit to Barcelona. Unfortunately, it's the most difficult to find, it's under Plaça Catalunya just outside El Corte Inglés – just look for the big 'i' signs on the pillars.

Carrer Ciutat, 2 is on the ground floor of the Ajuntament building on Plaça Sant Jaume and also offers a very complete service.

Plaça Portal de la Pau is situated close to the Columbus monument, and offers a more limited service of leaflets and guides.

Les Rambles, 99 only offers information on cultural events, and if you attempt to ask any other standard tourist questions, they'll direct you to one of the other offices.

If you want to take advantage of everything Barcelona has to offer, it's well-worth buying a Barcelona Card from either the Plaça Catalunya or the Carrer Ciutat tourist offices. These cards are valid from between two and five consecutive days, and allow you to use the metropolitan transport system free of charge as well as giving you entrance to the museums, attractions and discounts at restaurants. Prices start at €24 for a 2-day adult pass.

PALAU ROBERT

The tourist office you really should go to, though, is Palau Robert at Passeig de Gràcia, 107. This is a one-stop shop run by the Generalitat that will provide all the information you need for the whole of Catalonia – hotels, ski resorts, transport, blue flag beaches – you name it they've got it. They also put on some great exhibitions and regional showcases, so you can get a good idea of what you'll see before you go.

Contact Numbers: 012 (from inside Catalonia), (+34) 902 400 012 (from outside Catalonia)

EIXAMPLE

Population: 260,237

If you come blinking out into the light at Metro Catalunya and choose to look up the hill rather than down – the obvious choice for most – you might not be too impressed. The rather bland Plaça Catalunya is what you will see – fine if you want to feed pigeons, but no great shakes really. However, whilst expulsing breadcrumbs from your pockets or handbag, I suggest you make the tangential journey towards the top right hand corner of the square, and lo and behold, you'll find yourself at the bottom of Passeig de Gràcia, the time warp tunnel to Barcelona's recent Modernist past – a weird cross between Tolkien, Beatrix Potter and the Spice Girls.

The fact that L'Eixample houses the best concentration of Modernist architecture in the world is mainly due to the eccentric ideas of one man, Ildefons Cerdà, who would probably turn in his grave if he could see what became of his original concept. In 1859, Barcelona needed to grow, its people had begun to demolish the city walls which the Spanish government had built 150 years earlier and the Ajuntament called for designs for the new city. After many comings and goings, the plan that was chosen was Cerdà's, a socialist civil engineer who took the plight of Barcelona's working class very much to heart and drew up a simple grid system that would include public spaces, schools and hospitals and become a workers' utopia.

The fact that L'Eixample houses the best concentration of Modernist architecture in the world is mainly due to the eccentric ideas of Ildefons Cerdà

However, as soon as building started the monied classes decided to move out of their cramped quarters in the Barri Gòtic and around the port and began commissioning spacious new apartments and business addresses. The migration of money coincided, and probably stimulated, a new generation of architects, most notably Lluís Domènech i Montaner, Antoni Gaudí and Josep Puig i Cadafalch, who began to pepper the new barri with their fantastic creations. Many of their buildings are still in private hands, restricting your viewing to the outside, but turning L'Eixample into a huge urban museum around which it's a pleasure to wander.

The Eixample is still Barcelona's main shopping and business district, spreading out on either side of its two main thoroughfares, Passeig de Gràcia and Rambla de Catalunya, which run parallel to each other cutting northwest up the hill to Diagonal – just the other side of which is the Sagrada Familia. Most of what you will want to see can be found between these two streets with a slightly higher concentration in the Passeig de Gràcia direction in what is known as the Dreta de L'Eixample, or the right of the Eixample.

Gaudí's Sagrada Familia, Barcelona's most emblematic building, is still under construction to this day.

Further right above Avinguda Diagonal is the barri of the Sagrada Familia, most famous for Barcelona's most emblematic building, the Expiatory Temple of the Sagrada Familia, originally designed by Gaudí to purge the sins of the modern world and still under construction. Further down the hill is the little known Fort Pienc, which is more rundown and homely, and most likely to be visited for Barcelona's main bus station, L'Estació del Nord.

Back on Passeig de Gràcia again, if you walk in the opposite direction, L'Esquerra, or left, de L'Eixample starts once you've crossed Carrer Balmes. Without much of note in the way of architecture, this is still a really nice part of town with very good shopping that is much cheaper than on Passeig de Gràcia. There are also some great places to eat and in Luz de Gas, the barri has one of the coolest nightspots in the city. Perhaps this is because L'Antiga Esquerra has become home to an upwardly mobile gay community. Not that you would notice if you hadn't been told, but according to a friend of mine who lives there, there are not only gay bars and clubs, but gay plumbers, dentists and greengrocers as well. It's not at all in your face, though, and the area's atmosphere of convivial acceptance is one of the things that makes me proud to be a *Barcelonin*.

The barri on the other side of Carrer d'Urgell is more recent as until the early 20th century it was a heavy manufacturing neighbourhood. Some of the old factories have been dolled up and are in public use, but the nicest part is the Parc de L'Escorxador. This was built on the site of an old slaughterhouse and is home to Miró's alluring trencadis sculpture, Dona i Ocell, Woman and Bird.

If you double back to Carrer Rocafort and walk down the hill, you come to Sant Antoni. A particularly good place for buying furniture, strangely enough, and centred around the fine Mercat de Sant Antoni. This traditional iron girder market is even more authentic than the Boqueria, and also stages a great book and antique market on Sunday mornings. It's to here that kids flock from all over Barcelona to swap and complete their card collections. So if you see a group of them huddled in a circle and hear them muttering 'Tingui, Tingui, Falti', 'Got, Got, Not Got', you'll know you've seen a side of Barcelona that few people ever will.

Oficina d'Atenció al Ciutadà, Carrer Aragó, 328 Tel. 900 226 226

SANTS-MONTJUÏC

Population: 176,027

Given that it includes the port and the enormous Zona Franca industrial complex, Sants-Montjuïc is actually the largest district in Barcelona. However, unless you work in shipping or for a multinational based in Zona Franca, the only impression you'll have of this part of the district is as an eyesore on the right as you drive into the city from El Prat airport. The areas that people actually live in, though, are Poble Sec and Sants and the mountain of Montjuïc is another of those places that you'll come back to again and again.

The first impression you'll have of this part of the district is as an eyesore on the right as you drive into the city from El Prat airport.

How you get to the mountain all depends on where in the city you're based. When I lived in the Barri Gòtic, a day out on Montjuïc always meant catching the funicular from Poble Sec and coming out behind the old funfair. As the barri starts just at the end of Nou de la Rambla in the Raval, the Parallel end of Poble Sec was also a good place for late night drinking. Clubs like

Studio 54 and the Apollo, still a ravers' mecca, never got started till the early hours of the morning, and the bar next to El Molino variety theatre was where you had breakfast and got chatted up by transvestites.

Sants itself, apart from Sants Estació, the main railway station, has always remained a bit of a mystery to me. I know it was one of the main industrial barris of Barcelona in the 19th century. It's got some lovely little streets and a real village atmosphere of its own. Every time I have cause to visit, I always think that I should spend more time there but I never do. I suppose that's just because it's on the far side of the city and where I live in Sant Andreu is also a working-class post-industrial barri. If I didn't live where I do, though, I'd probably move to Sants.

A place I do frequent is the mountain of Montjuïc, but these days I always approach it from Metro Plaça Espanya, which is on the red line (so I can get there from home without having to change train). The walk up from the metro station is impressive. Flanked by buildings that hold a multitude of business fairs, Avinguda Reina Maria Cristina takes you to the foot of the mountain and the Palau Nacional, home of the fabulous Museu Nacional d'Art de Catalunya. A visit to MNAC takes a whole day, but assuming you're not as obsessive about medieval Catalan art as I am, you could also take in the Museu Arqueològic, the Fundació Miró and the Teatre Grec, which are all off to the left. For the faint-hearted, there's Mies van der Rohe's German Pavilion, the Poble Espanyol, which can only be described as a journey through Spanish architecture in miniature, and the Magic Fountains, whacky weird wonderful Barcelona at its best with choreographed water and light that grooves to anything from Abba to Mozart.

The Magic Fountains just up from Plaça Espanya at the foot of Montjuïc are one of the true delights of Barcelona. I've seen the show so many times over the last 20 years because I just can't let my visitors go home without them seeing them for themselves.

So you've been there for three days and you're hardly above sea level. Carry on up the hill and you'll reach the Olympic Ring, which was built for the 1992 Games. It's greener and more spacious here and you'll see why Barcelona considers it a much-needed source of oxygen. Look out for the Olympic Stadium, with its 1929 façade and intestines remodelled for 1992, the Palau Sant Jordi and Santiago Calatrava's communications tower.

The crowning glory of Montjuïc is its castle. Historically the site from which the Spanish army bombarded the stroppy *Barcelonins* with cannon balls whenever they got a little out of hand, it was returned to the Generalitat in 2006. It's now got a great military museum and in summer you can sit out until the early hours drinking and eating. Ominously, though, just over the crest of the hill is the cemetery, where the victims of Spanish repression under the Bourbons and Franco still lie in rest.

Oficina d'Atenció al Ciutadà, Creu Coberta, 104

A view of Barcelona from the steps outside the Museu Nacional d'Art de Catalunya that take you up from Plaça Espanya to Montjuïc.

93

LES CORTS

Population: 82,546

The district of Les Corts begins at Plaça Francesc Macià and runs along either side of the often opulent Avinguda Diagonal, and in much the same way as Barcelona's other districts it's more than it seems at first glance. It can be divided up into the barris of Les Corts and Pedralbes and the greener area known as La Maternitat and Sant Ramon, which is home to Camp Nou, FC Barcelona's cathedral of football.

To be perfectly honest, the historic centre of Les Corts is one of the parts of Barcelona I know least well. I've had cause to veer off that part of Avinguda Diagonal occasionally, generally in search of liquid refreshment, and I once worked at a language school on Josep Tarradellas, but it's never left a very deep impression. It seems a nice place to live with good bars, pubs and clubs and that's about it.

Pedralbes, though, is quite another thing, and is the part of Barcelona where the super-rich tend to live. Founded in 986, Pedralbes was originally known as Petras Albes or dawn stones, owing to the clear colour of the rock on which it is built. In 1327, Elisenda of Montcada, the fourth wife of Jaume II laid the first stone of the sublime Monastery of Pedralbes, considered one of the masterpieces of Gothic architecture and now home to part of the internationally famous Thyssen-Bornemisza art collection. Not surprisingly for such a select neighbourhood, many of the main streets are lined with sumptuous mansions surrounded by lush walled gardens. The privileged children of their owners also have it easy as the North Campus of Barcelona University is just round the corner.

Another of the privileges of living in Pedralbes is its proximity to Camp Nou. The Pedralbes crowd can be seen in the best seats far out of reach, both physically and financially, from down at heel football fans like you and me. I do have a claim to some upper-class Catalan pedigree, though. My daughter was born at the Hospital de la Maternitat on 20th December 1994.

Pedralbes is the part of Barcelona where the super-rich tend to live.

Oficina d'Atenció al Ciutadà, Plaça Comas, 18

SARRIÀ-SANT GERVASI

Population: 138,656

Sarrià-Sant Gervasi is the main point of entry to Barcelona's lungs, the delightfully wild conservation area on the Collserola mountain ridge. This is uptown Barcelona, in both senses of the word; it's not only at the top of the hill but also where the big money folks, *'la gent de bé'*, hang out. You can tell this by the fact that there are very few metro stations (the metro is a bit below the uptown boys and girls) and you have to move around using the Ferrocarrils – a kind of local train service which is definitely a cut above the metro or RENFE.

The best way to see the district is to get off the Ferrocarrils at Plaça Molina and start walking up Via Augusta. You'll walk past slick Muntaner, bourgeois Bonanova, slightly more rundown Tres Torres and finally wind up in the still delightful village-cum-suburb of Sarrià. If you continue walking you'll soon find yourself wandering up into the Collserola massif – there are a lot of toffs around these parts but you can't knock it really.

The part I know best is the bit closest to town because the British Council is at the top of Carrer Amigó within walking distance of Sant Gervasi and Bonanova; select neighbourhoods with select business premises for select clients who live in select residences, but also a congenial place to move about and work in.

Just out of walking distance is the one-time village of Sarrià, which according to records also dates back to the year 985. Originally the home to craftsmen and farmers in medieval times, it quickly became gentrified in the 19th century as big money *Barcelonins* bought first, or sometimes second, homes on the hills outside Barcelona. An indication of Sarrià's financial and political muscles is that whereas almost all the other villages outside Barcelona were incorporated by the city in 1897, Sarrià held out until 1921. It's still a lovely place and a good time to see it in its full glory is during its slightly genteel festa in the first week of October.

Barcelona seen from the funfair at the top of Tibidabo. It was here that the Devil reportedly tempted Christ with all the treasures of the world. The name comes from the Vulgar Latin *'haec tibi omnia dabo si cadens adoraveris me me'* – *'All this I will give you if you prostrate yourself before me.'*

Further up Collserola you come to Valvidrera, which nestles underneath Tibidabo, home to the funfair and the highest point of the Collserola massif. Once you're over the crest of the hills, you're really not in Barcelona any longer and you come to the glorious village of Les Planes. If I could choose, and had enough money in the bank, this is where I'd live. Les Planes combines everything; a short hop from a megacity but surrounded by luscious green forests. What more could anyone desire?

Oficina d'Atenció al Ciutadà, Carrer Anglí, 31

GRÀCIA

Population: 119,210

Gràcia is just cool. If you want to be cool, and I mean cool in the coolest possible way, go to Gràcia – you'll love it. Until the Eixample was built, Gràcia was a village on the outskirts of Barcelona, and the wonderful thing about it is that it still retains the village atmosphere whilst being in walking distance of the city centre – you can stride up the hill in the evening to sample its delights and then stumble down again half-cut back to wherever you're staying.

The old town begins at the top of Passeig de Gràcia, and is bordered roughly by Via Augusta to the west and the streets above the Sagrada Familia to the east, but the district is long and thin reaching up towards the Collserola ridge. Old Gràcia can be a little too trendy for its own good at times – it has traditionally been home to arty political types, students and the intelligentsia, but it's a also got a rough and ready traditional Catalan population, who will quickly put anyone in their place if they get too big for their boots.

There some great places to eat and some of the hottest nightclubs in town, but for me, the real delight is sitting out on a hot summer night swigging a beer on a terrace in one of its lovely squares – my personal favourites are Plaça del Sol and Plaça Rius i Taulet (otherwise known as Plaça del Rellotge – Clock square, because of the clock tower in the centre). If you happen to be around in the middle of August for the Festes de Gràcia, you won't be disappointed. Apart from the free concerts and all the usual stuff, they have a best-dressed street competition and every alleyway is decked with streamers and effigies turning them into fantastic grottos. The locals sit out and eat at trestle tables, drink flows freely, any resident with even minimal musical ability gets up to perform on a makeshift stage at one end and, in my experience, outsiders are always welcome.

Gràcia is just cool. If you want to be cool, and I mean cool in the coolest possible way, go to Gràcia – you'll love it.

The part above Travessera de Dalt and Plaça Lesseps, which permanently looks like a building site, is radically different and contains a number of mountainous parks. The most famous of these is Gaudí's Park Güell, which was originally planned as a garden city development, but failed to attract investors. Eusebi Güell's loss was Barcelona's gain because it shows Gaudí's talent at its most extreme, where the line between the organic architecture of plants and rocks becomes indistinguishable from the manmade. I always prefer to visit the park from Metro Vallcarca rather than Metro Lesseps, which involves a dusty trudge along Travessera de Dalt and an uphill climb to the park gates. From Vallcarca you can use mechanical escalators to get to the top of Muntanya Pelada, and then the visit to the park is all downhill, especially if you take the metro from Lesseps to get back home again.

Oficina d'Atenció al Ciutadà, C/ Francisco Giner, 46

HORTA-GUINARDO

Population: 169,739

Sadly, the hilly part of the district, once the ancient Valley of Horta is now known as the Vall d'Hebron, which brings little more to mind than Barcelona's main hospital of the same name. However, Carmel, La Teixonera, La Clota, La Vall d'Hebron, Sant Genís de Agudelles and Montbau form a scattered group of hilly barris that can loosely be called Horta. There's plenty of green round here, and a trip to the maze, the Laberint d'Horta, is a particularly convivial way to spend a morning.

Many of the populated areas began life as shantytowns, and although improved since the return of democracy, much still needs to be done.

There's also the hospital, some bits and bobs left over from the Olympics, and some nice old buildings, but architecturally much of the barri isn't much to write home about. One of the reasons for this is that the right-hand section of the Collserola ridge, in complete contrast to Pedralbes and the hills above Sarrià, became home to the immigrant overspill in the 1950s. Many of the populated areas began life as shantytowns, and although improved since the return of democracy, much needs to be done. This does mean, though, that areas have a certain other-worldliness that makes you think you are anywhere but Catalonia. Perhaps the Ajuntament hasn't invested in these barris because it believes that the advantages of living out in the hills outweigh the poor living conditions.

Closer to town is Guinardó, a barri that is much the same as many other inner-city Barcelona barris, apart from one incredible monument. The amazing modernist Hospital de Sant Pau was begun in 1902 by

Lluís Domènech i Montaner; a hospital like no other where art and architecture were conceived as part of the therapeutic process. It has to be seen to be believed, and if you're feeling a bit under the weather, a visit to Urgencies at Sant Pau is a certain pep to the metabolism.

Oficina d'Atenció al Ciutadà, Ronda Guinardó, 49

NOU BARRIS

Population: 165,368

One of the problems of Nou Barris, which means Nine Neighbourhoods, is that it lacks an historic centre and therefore is hard to pin down. Although it's probably the barri with fewest stops on any tourist agenda, like most of Barcelona, it's actually quite a nice place to live; built up in parts, rundown in others with a sizeable swathe of green that stretches out towards El Vallès.

My main point of argument with Nou Barris is that, if you count Vilapicina i la Torre Llobeta, Turó de la Peira, Porta, Can Peguera, La Prosperitat, La Nova Trinitat, La Guineueta, Canyelles, Verdun, Les Roquetes, Torre Baró and Ciutat Meridiana, you get eleven neighbourhoods not just nine, and the other day a nice man from the Ajuntament told me that, if you want to be pernickety about it, there are actually thirteen – just another of the mysteries of Nine Neighbourhoods.

If it hadn't been for first the building of the railway line out to central Catalunya Vella from Sant Andreu Arenal and later the inauguration of the Avinguda Meridiana, Barcelona's main road link to Northern Europe, most of Nou Barris wouldn't exist as a distinct entity. Most of it would still be part of Sant Andreu or Horta, both of which have a stronger sense of their own identity.

Living just on the other side of the Meridiana in Sant Andreu, I often have cause to explore the part of the barri that spreads out to the left of Passeig Fabra i Puig as you go up the hill; I worked at a language school in Virrei Amat, rehearsed with a band in Vilapicina, Plaça Soller is still good for a Sunday morning beer, the Can Dragó sports complex keeps the barri fit and my daughter tells me that the Heron City shopping complex is great for earrings.

Further out of the city, Nou Barris becomes greener and less inhabited. The only exception to this is the slightly marginal barri of Ciutat Meridiana, which stands behind the Torre Baró train station. I've never had call to get off and probably never will. This is immigrant Barcelona. Spanish, South American, North African and Sub-Saharan immigration leaves you with the sense that you're not really in Catalonia. It's hard to knock Nou Barris, though; perhaps its not on any tourist's agenda, perhaps the 'Catalans de sempre' think it's inhabited by people who don't belong here, but it's got a lively atmosphere and serves as a point of arrival for newcomers who will become New Catalans in due course.

As Nou Barris covers such a large area there are two offices. Oficina d'Atenció al Ciutadà, C/ Doctor Pi i Molist, 133 and Av Rasos de Peguera, 25

SANT ANDREU

Population: 141,154

As you drive past Sant Andreu, on your left along Avinguda Meridiana as you approach Barcelona, all you see is some faceless blocks of flats and you assume that what lies behind them is just as scratty and uninteresting as Nou Barris on the other side of the road. Nothing could be further from the truth. The high-rise buildings provide a protective screen for a village-cum-suburb of Barcelona the dates back to the late 10th century. It's not just chance that TV3's big soap opera El Cor de la Ciutat, the Heart of the City, is set in Sant Andreu; the district sums up the reality of life in Barcelona rarely seen by anyone except for those of us that live here.

The barris of Congrés, Navas, Bon Pastor, Baró de Viver and Trinitat Vella have got very little to get excited about; agreeable places to live and work, almost indistinguishable from neighbouring Nou Barris or Guinardó. The centre of the district, which consists of La Sagrera and Sant Andreu del Palomar, however, is quite a different matter. This is the heart of the barri and retains a strong sense of its own identity. In 1998, to commemorate the centenary of the district's 'annexation' by Barcelona, the locals dressed up in to turn of the century costume and made a tongue-in-cheek call for 'Independence and Autonomy'.

The faceless high-rise buildings provide a protective screen for a village-cum-suburb of Barcelona the dates back to the late 10th century.

The old part of the district is centred around Plaça Orfila where you'll find the mighty church of Sant Andreu del Palomar, the Ajuntament, the metro station and Sant Andreu Comtal train station. Here you're in walking distance of La Maquinista, now one of Barcelona's prime shopping centres, and Fabra i Coats, a particularly fine public library and park, both of which were once big factories dedicated to heavy industry and hark back to Sant Andreu's role, along with Sants, as one of the main manufacturing barris on the outskirts of the city.

Doubling back past the Ajuntament through Plaça del Comerç with Bar Versailles (highly recommended) on the corner, you come to tree-lined Gran de Sant Andreu, the main shopping street of the barri. If you turn left and continue down, you'll reach Sant Andreu's second centre, Passeig Fabra i Puig/Rambla Onze de Setembre. This Rambla is lined with bars where the locals sit out eating and drinking until the early hours, and provides the barri with its low-key but eminently convivial nightlife.

One of the best things about living in Sant Andreu is this conviviality that combines a village atmosphere with the cosmopolitan feel of the big city. Owing to its long-standing industrial base, the population is pretty evenly divided between Castilian-speakers and Catalans, but there is also a healthy presence of other nationalities - the other day I was watching the football with a Catalan friend when we were joined by fellow Barça fans from Morocco and Senegal. What's more we were being served by a Brazilian barmaid in a bar owned by a Spanish-speaking couple - he's from Andalusia and she's Aragonese - so things are happily multicultural here.

The strange thing is that, although people from very different cultures intermingle very freely, you are constantly aware that you are in Catalunya. This is because we have plenty of opportunities to celebrate the fact that we are all '*Andreuencs*' - the Festes del Barri in early December, Els Tres Tombs and the big parade on Kings' Day are all Sant Andreu affairs. We also enjoy Sant Jordi, Sant Joan and 11th September in our own way with the active participation of many local community groups - Els Diables de Sant Andreu are the life and soul of the party and local artists and painters find any excuse to exhibit on the Rambla just in front of our flat. My daughter attends the local scout group, 'El

Cau', my wife plays basketball with the Parents' Association at our daughter's school while my interests are served by SAT (Sant Andreu Teatre) and U.E. Sant Andreu, our local football team - we are currently riding high in the Third Division but even so we are the third best classified Barcelona team after Barça and Espanyol. Olé!

Sant Andreu is also particularly well-served by public transport. We have two mainline railway stations, the second biggest bus and coach station in Barcelona and metro stations Fabra i Puig and Sant Andreu will get you into the centre of the city in less than 20 minutes. When the new metro station on Onze de Setembre and the high-speed AVE station in La Sagrera are complete, Sant Andreu will take over from Sants as the neuralgic centre of Barcelona as far as transport is concerned. Hopefully, this won't upset the happy balance we have here, though – we're already used to day-trippers dropping in to take advantage of our excellent shopping facilities at La Maquinista, Heron City and Hipercor.

To be honest, there is very little bad I can say about Sant Andreu. Although, being a country boy, I sometimes get tired of the pollution, noise and stress that are part and parcel of city life. I wish there were more green spaces – more parks, allotments where I could grow vegetables and more open spaces where kids could play and kick a ball about. However, unless I win the lottery, I can't see myself leaving my home on Onze de Setembre in the heart of Sant Andreu – El Cor de la Ciutat!

Oficina d'Atenció al Ciutadà, Plaça Orfila, 1 and Carrer Juan de Garay, 116-118

Our local church of Sant Andreu del Palomar is quite impressive for a working class barri.

SANT MARTÍ

Population: 218,004

Twenty years ago I wouldn't have had very much to say about Sant Martí. A hundred years earlier it had been the village of Sant Martí del Provençals but its historic centre was pretty much destroyed by the building of Avinguda Meridiana and Plaça de les Glòries at the end of the 19th century. Its only saving grace was the delightful Rambla of the working-class barri of Poblenou, which incidentally was where my wife was born.

These days, however, Sant Martí is a different kettle of fish. The Rambla de Poblenou is still there and as lovely as ever, but now instead of leading down to a splurge of rundown and disused factories which blocked Barcelona off from the sea, it takes you directly to the beach.

Sant Martí was probably the district that benefited most from the urban renewal programme that began in the run-up to Barcelona's 1992 Olympic Games, and has not stopped since. What were once industrial slums are now some of the finest areas of the city. The seafront starts at the Port Olímpic and continues with the beaches of Nova Icària, Bogatell, Mar Bella and Nova Mar Bella, all of which are backed by parks and green spaces. The finishing touch to the barri came in 2004 when Barcelona hosted the Fòrum de les Cultures and needed an exhibition space. There was still a little bit of Sant Martí to be done up, so where Diagonal meets the sea, Diagonal Mar was built and the Fòrum Barcelona 2004 space was constructed to hold the conference. It's now a great place to go and watch free concerts and cultural activities in the summer – if you start suffering from cultural overkill, you can always go to the beach and get unculturally sunburnt.

Oficina d'Atenció al Ciutadà, Plaça Valentí Almirall, 1

GREATER BARCELONA

I've got no idea what the population of the City of London is, but we can't be talking about that many people. Greater London, though, is pretty big. Something similar occurs with Barcelona – the City of Barcelona has about 1.5 million inhabitants, but if you include Greater Barcelona the population explodes to some 4 million.

The Satellite Towns of Badalona, Hospitalet, Santa Coloma and Sant Adrià, which are all in the Barcelonès comarca, are really the fourth Barcelona. The Barri Gòtic goes back at least two thousand years, the Eixample a respectable 150, and villages likes Gràcia, Sant Andreu or Sants became part of the metropolis at the turn of the 20th century. These outer lying towns, though, were jerry-built in the 60s and 70s as a response to massive Andalusian immigration under Franco, and still suffer from a degree of stigma; part of the big city, yet somehow not.

Twenty years ago these places were full of 'lo-lailos' and 'quillos' (pejorative terms for the generally uneducated and uncultured immigrants). However, their children have grown up as New Catalans and money has been invested in making them nicer places to live. A lot of work needs to be done, but Greater Barcelona is beginning to get green spaces and museums, and with a little patience some real architectural and cultural gems can be found. Furthermore, as they are on the edge of the city, the countryside or the beaches are often within easy reach. So in some ways, you get both the best and the worst of the big city – high population density, kick ass city centre, rundown housing estates, close to the mountains.

BADALONA

Population: 217,663

The train pulls into the slightly scruffy Badalona station – the journey only takes eight minutes, and this is not quite a Barcelona beach but it's not quite the Costa del Maresme either. With 4.8 km of coastline, Badalona is the northern seafront of the Barcelonès comarca. Refined, it isn't but it does have a certain charm.

Badalona is a city with a population of nearly 220,000 people, the majority of whom migrated here from Andalusia in the 60s – or their parents did at least. It's a 'Viva la Pepa' kind of place – ghetto blasters playing loud techno-flamenco on the beach, young Spaniards rolling joints, asking for a light and then walking over your towel and kicking sand in your face on their way to the sea. I personally can only put up with Badalona beach for a few minutes, so I always end up going for a walk (and a beer somewhere, more than likely!)

I really like strolling over the railroad tracks, past the McDonald's on the corner and up into the old town. The buildings take the heat out of the sun, and you can pick up a soothing ice-cream on your way up the pedestrianised shopping street. By the time, I get into Badalona's medieval heart, I'm full of good intentions about visiting churches and museums, but as I've left the wife and daughter on the beach and there's no one around to give me a hard time, I generally sidle into a bar, read the football paper and down a couple of beers.

By that time, 2 o'clock is approaching and I'm beginning to feel a bit peckish. I walk down the hill again, feeling cool as the stone buildings extract the heat from the air around one. Then the glare of the sun suddenly hits, the floppy red breasts of topless housewives leave an imprint on my retina and the blare of techno-flamenco threatens to burst my eardrums. 'Time for lunch?' I blurt. My already-red wife and daughter nod, get dressed and then we go for something to eat at a terrace restaurant along the Passeig Marítim. In culinary terms the meal's nothing special, but it's cheap and it's worth it for the vibe.

It's easy to put down Badalona but the city has one other great thing going for it, and that is its basketball team, La Penya. Everyone has a secret love of La Penya; they come from a suburb but are capable of competing with Barça's basketball team on equal terms. A healthy situation – Visca la Penya!

Ajuntament de Badalona, Plaça de la Vila, 1 Tel. 93 483 26 00 *www.badalona.cat*

HOSPITALET

Population: 260,041

Twelve and a half square kilometres of schizophrenia, located on the northern bank of the River Llobregat, hemmed in by Barcelona, Esplugues, Cornellà and El Prat. That's Hospitalet, or L'H as its municipal spin doctors are wont to call it these days. The city's basic problem is that, in comparison with Barcelona, it's got a bad image, and even worse, although at 260,000 inhabitants, it's a fairly important city in its own right, people often assume it's just an extension of Barcelona.

Given that Hospitalet dates back until at least 400BC, this seems a little unfair. It didn't really get going until the twelfth century when the barri of Santa Eulàlia and Torre Blanca, now known as the barri del Centre, were founded. Hospitalet seems to have been relatively rural for the next five hundred years but started to grow again as the textile boom and the Industrial Revolution hit Catalonia in the 18th century, and really began to explode in the early 20th century when it was hit by mass immigration from southern Spain. It was then that Hospitalet's identity problems began and after becoming a city in 1925, it became known as a 'No Go' area for Catalans when the immigrants who had come to work on the construction of the Barcelona metro erected signs claiming 'Murcia starts here' whilst showing a stubborn refusal to learn the local language. Things went from bad to worse in the 1960s and 70s when Andalusians were shipped in en masse and the population more than tripled. Hospitalet's image as the least Catalan of Catalan cities became a truism that was etched in stone.

Recent caricatures of *Hospitalencs* have started from the timeworn cliché but have been forced to change tack. Novelist Matthew Tree starts his journey in search of Catalan culture in Hospitalet expecting not to find it, and although he leaves with reservations, he definitely finds a pluricultural angle on what it is to be Catalan that one can do nothing but celebrate. Even more poignant was José Cabacho's portrayal of Sebas, the Catalan-speaking waiter from Bar Sport whose love of life was only equalled by his love of fried eggs and chorizo. No character has sailed so closely against wind of accepted bourgeois Catalan culture as Sebas. He rang so true, he represented hope, and ten years on, his heirs are going to University. Hospitalet, Posa't guapa!

Hospitalet's image as the least Catalan of Catalan cities became a truism that was etched in stone.

There's no point in concealing it but I think that Hospitalet is one of the success stories of a new Catalonia; buildings are going up, scumbag ghettos are getting prettier, the Farga's becoming a cultural point of reference as a conference venue, Gran Via 2 is a pretty sexy shopping complex. Hospitalet is never going to figure highly in any tourist guide but if you wind up working for a multinational with offices in Zona Franca and company apartments in Hospitalet, you can count your lucky stars. Oh, and by the way, don't forget to have a caña and a plate of huevos con chorizo on me.

Ajuntament de L'Hospitalet. Plaça. de l'Ajuntament, 11 Tel. 934.029.400 *www.l-h.es*

BARCELONA PROVINCE

It's really difficult to work out where Barcelona ends and the rest of the province begins. According to 2005 figures, the city of Barcelona has a population of a little over one a half million, but the inhabitants of its urban sprawl number at least four million, more than half of Catalonia's population. Given such a high density, there are parts for which 'ugly' might be considered a compliment and 'truly hideous' a slightly more accurate description.

However, once you get away from the dominating throb of the Catalan capital's industrial belt, the oppressive atmosphere changes to light and beauty. A trip down the coast to Sitges or Vilanova i la Geltrú, a visit to the awe-inspiring mountain and monastery of Montserrat, a long hike across the plain of Vic finishing with a relaxed lunch in the region's medieval capital or a gruelling climb up Tagamanent, the highest point of the nearby Montseny mountains, will all be wonderfully rewarding. So check out of your Barcelona hotel, get in the hire car or on public transport and explore!

Once you get away from the dominating throb of the Catalan capital's industrial belt, the oppressive atmosphere changes to light and beauty.

GRANOLLERS

Population: 59.047

Granollers is capital of the Vallès Oriental, and one of those towns whose sleepy present hides a turbulent past. Apparently, there have been *Granollerencs* for about 4,000 years but the town didn't achieve much importance until 1044 when the name Granularios Subteriore first appears in the record books. The next few centuries seem to have been ones of relative prosperity punctuated by occasional wars, in which Granollers took a decidedly pro-Catalan stance; the Guerras dels Segadors, les Remences and el Francès along with a number of Carlist uprisings in the 19th century have all left their mark on Granollers.

Bombarded by Italo-German bombers during the Civil War, the town like many others suffered repression under the Franco regime but the end of the dictatorship also brought a demographic increase due to immigration, which was not quite so massive as in towns closer to Barcelona. Since Franco's death in 1975, Granollers has settled into sleepy prosperity being the commercial centre of a sprawling industrial zone, and its central square, La Porxada, is one of the loveliest in central Catalonia.

Granollers also has a particularly good Festa Major, which it hosts in the last week of August. The celebration is based on a bet set between two tile makers in 1897 to see who could make the most tiles in one day. I don't know who won but these days the city divides into two groups, Els Blancs (the Whites) and Els Blaus (the Blues) in commemoration of the colour of the tiles, and much fun is to be had. If you decide to go, you should stop for a meal at the excellent Fonda Europa and it might be worth dropping off your CV at Cambridge School (www.cambridgeschool.com), which is just behind La Porxada and one of the best language schools outside Barcelona.

Ajuntament de Granollers, Plaça de la Porxada 6 Tel. 938 426 610 *www.granollers.cat*

CIRCUIT DE CATALUNYA

If you're into Formula 1 or motorbikes, Granollers might be a good place to stay as it's just five minutes away from Montmeló, where the Circuit de Catalunya is located. This motor racing circuit is probably the most important in Spain (with the permission of Jerez) and generally hosts the Spanish Grand Prix, major motorbike races as well as rallies, demolition derbies and the like. For information about upcoming events visit *www.circuitcat.com*

SABADELL

Population: 200,905

Sabadell is another place that is heir to an extraordinary amount of history. The town claims to go back to 5,000BC but in reality Sabadell's pre-history probably amounts to little more than a few Iberians waiting around for the Romans to arrive. As with so many other towns it enters the records in the early 11th century, when central Catalonia was being repopulated following the Moorish invasion. By all accounts, though, it didn't really get going until much later. From the 16th century, it had been a centre for the textile industry so when the Industrial Revolution came it entered a boom period and its population began to grow. A reflection of Sabadell's prosperity is that it is still the seat of two important banks, the Caixa d'Estalvis de Sabadell and Banc Sabadell.

These days Sabadell is one of Catalonia's nicer industrial towns, which although hit by mass immigration under Franco retains a clear sense of its own identity. The outskirts are a bit characterless, but the old town is particularly pleasant with a ramshackle feel that harks back to its long history. I particularly like some of the old Industrial Revolution buildings and the surprising number of Modernist gems, which were designed by mainly second division architects but are delightful nonetheless.

Sabadell's pre-history probably amounts to little more than a few Iberians waiting around for the Romans to arrive.

It's a particularly dynamic town and by all accounts an excellent place to live. The Festa Major always begins on the first Friday of September and lasts a week, but there's a lot more to enjoy throughout the year with each barri celebrating its own festa and quite a few musical events as well; Sabadell even boasts its own symphony orchestra. My overriding impression of Sabadell, which goes back over a decade and might well be a little out of date, are of relaxed bar crawls through the winding backstreets of the old town – an altogether pleasurable experience.

Ajuntament de Sabadell Plaça de Sant Roc, 1 - 08201 Sabadell - Tel 93 745 31 00 *www.sabadell.cat*

TERRASSA

Population: 200.000

Although these days it is probably not as obviously attractive as its sister Sabadell, Terrassa has a lot to offer as a place to live and the town does have an impressive, and well-documented, history.

It is really worth spending some time to scratch below Terrassa's superficial impression as an industrial city.

The Roman city of Ègara (Municipium Flavium Egara) was located around the church of Sant Pere and the seasonal river Vallparadis, an area where not only Roman ruins but also remains of an older Iberian settlement can be seen. Like many other Catalan towns, Terrassa grew into a walled city in Medieval times and expanded and prospered throughout the following centuries. Along with Barcelona and Sabadell, it became one of the major centres of the textile industry during the Industrial Revolution and the fact that the Museu Nacional de la Ciència i de la Tècnica, the National Science and Technology Museum, is located in Terrassa reflects its importance. Another significant corollary to Terrassa's wealth in the late 19th century is its incredible Modernist architecture, the richness of which is reflected in the words of Eugeni d'Ors, who described Terrassa as the 'Athens of Catalonia.'

Admittedly, the demographic growth caused by the mass immigration of the 50s and 60s has somewhat tarnished Terrassa's beauty but first impressions are not always what they seem and it is really worth spending some time to scratch below Terrassa's superficial impression as an industrial city. For those so inclined, perhaps the best way to get to know Terrassa is through its vibrant music scene. The Nova Jazz Cava on Ptge

Tete Montoliu s/n is one of the best venues in Spain and regularly features big name international jazz stars as well as home-grown talent, and throughout March Terrassa hosts a magnificent jazz festival which showcases Latin jazz at its best without forgetting swing and bebop. Information about what's going down in Terrassa can be found on *www.jazzterrassa.org*

Ajuntament de Terrassa, Raval de Montserrat 14, 08221 Terrassa Tel. 93 739 70 60 *www.terrassa.cat*

Oficines de Turisme, Raval de Montserrat, 14 and Rambla d'Ègara, 270

CATALONIA AND COTTON

In the second half of the 19th century, Catalonia's textile industry was third in the world after the US and Britain, and as a result, being the financial centre of the region, Barcelona was dubbed the 'Manchester of the Mediterranean'. Much of the actual production, though, was based in Sabadell and Terrassa, who proudly refer to themselves as the 'Leeds and Bradford of the Mediterranean' in municipal records of the time.

Being a northerner myself, I find something strangely satisfying about this description. To get to Leeds and Bradford from Manchester, you have to cross the Pennines and there they are, an industrial anachronism set against the backdrop of the Yorkshire Moors and Dales. Similarly, to get to Sabadell and Terrassa from Barcelona, you go over the Collserola Ridge, down into an industrial valley that a century ago must have been as grimy as any industrial town in Britain, but beyond lies the unspoilt beauty of El Vallès. It's not surprising I feel at home around these parts.

SANT CUGAT

Population: 73,439

For some reason Sant Cugat is regarded as a highly desirable place to live and its inhabitants considered rather well-to-do. This is because it's both close enough to Barcelona for its inhabitants to take full advantage of everything the city has to offer whilst being far enough away to be able to sleep peacefully at night. Its location in the middle of the Collserola is also a great advantage making Sant Cugat, in short, a commuter heaven. An interesting statistic that the town likes to brag about is that there is one tree per 2.16 inhabitants.

The town also boasts a real piece of architectural finery in its Monastery, which dates back to 878 and during the reign of the interestingly-named Frankish king Louis the Stutterer was the most important abbey in the County of Barcelona. What you can see today is the Benedictine abbey that was built in the 12th century and combines early Romanesque and later Gothic features; it's pure poetry in stone.

Sant Cugat also has more than its fair share of excellent festes. The Festa Major takes place around 29th June to celebrate Sant Pere, the town's patron saint, and there's also a very lively Festa de Tardor, or Autumn Festival, during the first weekend of November. My favourite, though, is the Festa del Llibre Gegant, the Festival of the Giant Book, in early May when all the town's children are invited to write a story which is published in a necessarily gigantic book.

Ajuntament de Sant Cugat, Plaça de la Vila, 1 Tel. 93 565 70 00 *www.santcugat.org*

Tourist Office, Plaça Octavia, S/N Tel. 93 675 99 52

SITGES

Population: 23.590

Internationally, Sitges is probable best-known as being the gay capital of Spain and host to the International Cinema Festival of Catalonia, the theme of which is fantasy and science fiction – and Sitges given its history and liberalism is not at all a bad place to hold it.

To Catalans, it is more famous for its exuberant Carnaval in early spring; this takes place on the infamous Carrer del Pecat – the Street of Sin - and is not to be missed. It's an out and out gay/transvestite event to which grandparents take their grandchildren, and where local farmers can be seen talking football (I presume) to drag queens.

But Sitges is not only well-endowed sexually, it is also a delightful place to visit. The Passeig Marítim extends for 3 km along the seafront and overlooks some of the nicest beaches within easy reach of Barcelona. At the end of the Passeig, there are a set of steps that take you up to the Old Town and the majestic 12th century church of Sant Bartolomeu i Santa Tecla, the museum and the Palau Maricel.

For me, though, the real delight of Sitges comes as you walk down the hill towards the Sant Sebastià beach with its classy seafront bars and restaurants. This part of town is also home to the Cau Ferrat, now a museum, which once belonged to the Modernist painter Santiago Rusinyol who celebrated his famous Modernist parties there. His purchase of two El Greco paintings, which are still housed in the museum, was apparently the cause of much debauchery a century ago.

Apart from Carnaval, a good time to visit is for the Festa Major of Sant Bartomeu, which is on 23rd August at the height of the summer season. Even more lovely, though, is Corpus Christi, when the streets are decorated by carpet-like flower mosaics, which have to be tiptoed across in order to get from one side of the street to the other.

Sitges is a lovely place – it's quiet and cultural with lovely beaches and great places to eat. If you go with the kids, though, be sure you don't inadvertently set your packed lunch down on the gay nudist section of the beach!

Ajuntament de Sitges Pl. Ajuntament, sn. Tel. 938 117 600 *www.sitges.cat*

VIC

Population: 40,000

Vic, it has to be said, is amongst my favourite places in Catalonia. It manages to mix oodles of history with upbeat modernity, and a cosmopolitan atmosphere with a strong sense of tradition. It's also one of a number of towns that stakes a strong claim to being the cradle of Catalonia.

With so many young people around, Vic is also well-known for its fairs and festes.

Vic began life as Ausa, the capital of an Iberian tribe called the Ausetans, who gave their name to the comarca of which Vic is now capital, Osona. Later colonised by the Romans, Vic's location on the Plain of Vic, the heart of central Catalonia's fertile flatlands, has always been essential to its prosperity, and its agricultural roots are still to be savoured in its wonderful array of local sausages, which can be bought direct from the pig farmers at the Tuesday and Saturday markets in the main square.

The markets in the old Medieval town centre seem to sum up all that is Vic. The streets are full of young and old, the market traders sell everything from local honey to pirate CDs. All this occurs in atmosphere that is strongly Catalan but also includes a healthy racial mix, because Vic seems extremely confident of both its past and its future.

The town was once seat of one of the most powerful bishoprics in Catalonia, and a sign of its historical importance is its amazing Museu Episcopal, which houses a collection of Romanesque art only equalled by the MNAC in Barcelona. The bishopric was always an important seat of learning and research, and this tradition is continued by the University of Vic, the only Catalan university located in a town of such diminutive size.

Not surprisingly, with so many young people around, Vic is also well-known for its fairs and festes. The real time to visit is in mid-September, when the Mercat de la Música Viva de Vic takes place. The MMVV is the trade fair for the Catalan music industry, but while a lot of business obviously goes on, the town is turned into one massive concert hall. There's always a strong Catalan bias but the MMVV is becoming increasingly international, with many Spanish and British acts making a play for the very healthy Catalan music market. If you go, you certainly won't be disappointed by this 24/7 feast of music, fun and festa.

Ajuntament de Vic, C. Ciutat, 1 Tel. 938 862 100 *www.vic.cat*

GIRONA PROVINCE

The Costa Brava, or Rugged Coast, stretches from Blanes, which is about 60km north of Barcelona to Port Bou on the French border. With its wooded coves, tall cliffs, charming beaches and deep blue water that glistens under the Mediterranean sun, this was once the most beautiful part of the Spanish coastline. It's still like this in parts – the northern section retains its local feel and scenic beauty, and is mainly visited by Catalans or French tourists from just across the border – but speaking as a lover of traditional Catalan ways, I am sometimes a little dismayed at the effects that 30 years of mass tourism have had on the southern part of the coast. However, it all depends on what you are after, and one cannot deny that resorts such as Lloret, Blanes and Platja d'Aro offer an excellent service to the international tourist in search of sun, sea and sand.

The southern string of resorts begins at Blanes, which, were it not for the seafront, could easily be mistaken for a suburb of Barcelona. Tossa de Mar offers all the tourist stuff, but also boasts a lovely old town and medieval walls which is as fine as anything you will see in Catalonia. I have a particular soft spot for Sant Feliu de Guíxols, and Lloret really is a matter of taste – it's brash and tacky, but if you're looking to deepen your tan and a loud, late, libidinous nightlife, then you won't be disappointed.

The remaining two thirds of the coastline beyond Palamós can be truly lovely, and have only been spoilt by the excesses of the property developers in places. From here on you will find apartments and villas rather than big tourist hotels. The beaches and villages close to the inland town of Palafrugell are still wonderfully scenic. Moving north, there is the ancient Greek site of Empúries, which is in walking distance from L'Escala, a satisfyingly reasonable resort in itself, and the rural and fairly isolated hinterland of the large bay, the Golf de Roses – much of this area is now protected and is home to a nature reserve, the Parc Natural dels Aiguamolls de l'Empordà.

Roses itself is the last of the Costa Brava's massive tourist developments, but is saved by an excellent beach, and is a great option if you want to combine sun and nightlife with quieter pursuits. Finally, the last stretch just south of the French border, which includes Cadaqués, Port de la Selva, Llançà and Port Bou, is still gorgeous – a five-minute walk from the main beach in each of these towns will take you to secluded coves that will give you an idea of what the whole of this coastline must have been like before the developers moved in. Furthermore, for the culturally-minded, just inland, you are within easy reach of the magnificent medieval monastery of Sant Pere de Rodes, and the Alt Empordà's capital, Figueres, where Salvador Dalí was born and established his superb surrealist museum.

Just like many towns along the coast Llançà has some fine beaches, a marina and a working fishing industry.

GIRONA

Population: 81,220

The ancient walled city of Girona stands like a fortress on a hill overlooking the River Onyar. Since it was founded by the Romans and given the name Gerunda, the site has been fought over for centuries. It was briefly under Moorish control during the 8th century, but was re-conquered by the Franks in 785, and so can stake a very valid claim to be the cradle of medieval Catalonia. By the 18th century the city had been besieged on 20 occasions, and in the 19th century, it earned itself the nickname 'Immortal' after surviving five sieges. These days, however, Girona exudes calm and tranquility, despite the fact that it is served by Catalonia's second largest airport – Immortal Girona is just as capable of beating back marauding Costa Brava-bound tourists as it was of holding out against Moors, Visigoths, and French and Castilian invaders.

There are two overriding images I have of Girona. The first is of the multicoloured houses that back on to the River Onyar as it winds its way through the city, and the second is of the sublime Parc de la Devesa. By day the park is a cool retreat from the hot sun, and by night, particularly in summer, it becomes an oasis more angled towards food, drink and culture. Throughout the summer months, it becomes host to a plethora of bars and restaurants under canvas that all seem to be the centre of some kind of performance, be it musical or theatrical, and a semi-intoxicated night in one of the park bars is just the best way to let the heat of a day's sunbathing ooze from your skin.

Girona's old town is also a cool escape from stresses of the nearby Costa Brava. Its Gothic Cathedral, which was built from the 11th to the 17th centuries, is particularly magnificent, and its nave is the widest Gothic religious arch in the world. Gaudí considered the Cathedral of Girona to be one of the essential pieces of architecture in Spain, and when you view some his own gravity-defying arches, it's easy to see where he took his inspiration from.

Other integral parts of any time spent should be a visit to El Call, one of the oldest Jewish quarters in Europe, and a walk round the walls, some parts of which date back to the reign of Charlemagne in the 9th century.

Immortal Girona is just as capable of beating back marauding Costa Brava-bound tourists as it was of holding out against Moors, Visigoths, and French and Castilian invaders.

Not surprisingly, Girona has a particularly lively cultural scene hosting Film, Theatre and Cartoon festivals in the autumn when the weather is still pleasant. The town's Festa Major is Sant Narcis, which begins in the last week of October, when although the weather's beginning to get a little less predictable, there's always lots to do.

Ajuntament de Girona, Plaça del Vi, 1 Tel. 972 419 010 *www.ajuntament.gi*

I often take the train from my home in Barcelona up to the Costa Brava, where my wife has family. I'm always sorely tempted to get off at Girona and revisit one of the loveliest cities in Catalonia, but what would my mother-in-law say if I didn't show up for lunch?

CADAQUÉS

Population: 2,623

Cadaqués is one of the most delightful places on the northern stretch of the Costa Brava. It is only accessible by a steep winding road that meanders through the surrounding hills, and so retains a peaceful air of isolation. I have always been charmed by the box-like whitewashed houses that line the narrow hilly streets. With its tree-lined promenade and rocky bays on either side of the harbour, which is still a working fishing port, it can only be described as truly picturesque. In summer, it's lovely but it's even better out of season – you can sit with your carajillo in the glass-fronted Casino de l'Amistat, a kind of bar-cum-cultural centre on the seafront, and watch the boats come in, safe in the knowledge that the bitter Tramuntana wind will only bite if one of the domino-playing pensioners forgets to close the door.

In the 1940s, Salvador Dalí built a house at Port Lligat, on the outskirts of the town, attracting an itinerant community of artists and wannabes, so despite being a little too trendy for it's own good and a sometimes annoying proliferation of BMWs, the town is full of fascinating little private galleries. Both the Museu Perrot-Moore and the Museu Municipal d'Art show work by local artists mostly inspired by the spectacular coastline, and are a must for art lovers.

Given that the beaches are small and pebbly, and I'm not one for sunbathing anyway, I strongly recommend finding a quiet spot for a quiet beer in the area around the late-Gothic church, l'Església Santa Maria, which was built between the 16th and 18th centuries. Apart from its musty calm, it boasts some gorgeous baroque murals on wood designed in 1725 by Jacint Moretó and finished by Pau Costa in 1788.

As evening falls, you can walk back up through town and eat in a variety of atmospheric restaurants that range from reasonable to extortionate in price – so make sure you check the menu outside before you sit down. After a few drinks and an excellent meal, I'm sure you'll reach the same conclusion as me – Cadaqués is well-worth a visit.

Ajuntament de Cadaqués, Carrer Silví Rahola, 2 Tel. 972 258 200 *www.cadaques.org*

FIGUERES

Population: 34,047

If it weren't for the fact that my wife's family are all scattered around the Alt Empordà, meaning lunches and overnight stays that are difficult to get out of, I know exactly how I'd go about getting to know the northern Costa Brava – I'd get off the train from Barcelona at Figueres, find a cheap hotel and use the town as my base for exploring the region.

Figueres is a lovely provincial town with charming central Rambla, lots of things to see and do, and if you want reasonably-priced Catalan menus del dia, you just have to explore the backstreets. From its laidback rhythm, though, you'd never guess that it's home to one of the most popular museums in Spain – El Museu Dalí.

Salvador Dalí was born in Figueres in 1904, giving his first exhibition in the town at the tender age of just fourteen and later going on to to international renown. In 1974, he came back home and decided to set up a museum in the old municipal theatre. However, being Dalí this wouldn't be just any old museum but a complete work of art in itself. If you expect to find some of his famous works, you'll be disappointed, but I'm not joking a visit to this Disneyland-out-of-Hell will mark you for life.

I particularly like the Cadillac with human (not live ones of course) occupants covered in snails (which are alive!) – if you put a coin in the slot the figures get drenched with water and you make the snails happy. There's a totem pole made out of tyres with a boat and an umbrella on top, the debauched Mae West which you view through a mirror, a complete life-sized orchestra, skeletons crop up in odd places, a bed with fish tails plus, in comparison with what's gone before, some rather dull surrealist sculptures and paintings. There's no end to madness – kids (both big and small) just love it.

Dalí's theatre-museum – the building itself, topped by a huge metallic dome and decorated with luminous egg shapes, is the first exhibit, and once inside things go from mad to worse.

If you want round off a really great family day, after a quiet beer, you can go on to the Museu dels Joguets, the toy museum, and on a more serious note there's the Museu de l'Empordà, with local Roman finds and exhibits from local artists. Not to be missed is the huge seventeenth century Castell de Sant Ferran.

Ajuntament de Figueres, Plaça de l'Ajuntament, 12 Tel. 972032200 *www.ddgi.cat/webfigue*

CAGANERS

Apparently, the Museu dels Joguets in Figueres is the proud host of the largest collection of Caganers in the world, and is definitely worth a visit just so you can see how weird the Catalans are for yourself. But what are Caganers? Well, they're small figures that are normally dressed in traditional Catalan regalia – black trousers, a white shirt and a red boina – and are placed in the Nativity Scenes at Christmas in homes across the country. Fine, you might think, a folkloric figure to add to the Jesus, Mary and Joseph, the shepherds, kings and farm animals. But, the Caganer is something different – he's always placed at the back, he's got his trousers down and a large turd is emanating from his backside. What an earth is he doing in such a spiritual setting? He's having a good old crap, of course, and when you've got to go, even the birth of Christ isn't an adequate reason to divert the call of nature.

In actual fact, the Caganer is an ancient figure, who symbolises the fertilisation of the land, and his presence at the birth of Christ is an almost pagan recognition that the law of nature is still the ultimate rule. Modern Catalans, though, are also inclined to see the funny side, and the figure has become a kind of skit on the modern world – hence the collection in Figueres. There are Caganers made in the likeness of many people in the public domain – Ronaldinho, the President of the Generalitat, the Spanish President, George Bush etc. What's strange is that if you are seen in a positive light by Catalan society, having a Caganer in your image is the highest compliment. Warlike American presidents and sporting rivals should beware, though – if they don't like you, being made into a Caganer is the most belittling of insults.

OLOT

Population: 31,932

As capital of the volcanic Garrotxa region, Olot boasts an undeniable charm. Fertile, impressive, creative, obsessive; there's a lot to Olot. The town itself is lovely, with its calm pedestrianised streets, excellent shops and lovely bars but it is Olot's setting that makes it so special. In the centre of the Garrotxa nature reserve, the town is an ideal base from which to visit this region of fortunately now extinct volcanoes.

One of the best ways to get an idea of Olot, past and present, is to visit El Museu Comarcal de la Garrotxa, which houses a fine collection of local painters who became known as the Olot School because their work incorporates scenes and perspectives from La Garrotxa that were later to influence Catalan painting as a whole.

The town is an ideal base from which to visit this region of fortunately now extinct volcanoes.

The Festa Major, les Festes del Tura, in the second week of September seem solidly Catalan in all aspects and, given that Olot is such a pleasing place to be, is sure to be worth a visit. This is a 'big cheese' festival in which one of Catalonia most emblematic towns shows off its cultural excellence, its culinary delights and its 'collons' at their *Olotin* best.

Ajuntament d'Olot, Passeig Bisbe Guillamet, 10 Tel 972 279 100 *www.olot.org*

PERALADA

Population: 1,500

Built on a small hill in the centre of the Alt Empordà comarca, Peralada is a delight. Its narrow streets, its lovely museums, the cloister of Sant Domènec and the parks and gardens of its curious casino-castle all add up to make Peralada the ideal place to spend a summer afternoon or early evening, and if you're feeling peckish, make sure to stop off for some seafood served at the popular restaurant-terraces on the edge of the old town. Particularly in summer, this is one of the places to see the local Catalan bourgeoisie at their best. Beware the noise, though; the clinking of plates, the snapping of lobster claws and the sometimes ostentatious rattling of jewellery are all signs that, although the prices are reasonable, you're definitely dining with the best.

Founded in 500BC by the Iberian Indiketes tribe, Peralada really came into its own during the period of Carolingian domination in the 8th and 9th centuries at which point it became one of the capitals of Medieval Catalonia. The truth is that the town still seems trapped in a bygone age, and little appears to have happened there since its time of glory. It was sacked on a number of occasions and its trials and tribulations are faithfully recounted in its small museum dedicated to Peralada's most illustrious son, Ramon Muntaner. Muntaner left his home town after a period of violence in the early 14th century and joined a group of Catalan mercenaries called the Almogàvers. In the name of the Crown of Aragon, the Almogàvers conquered southern Greece and made inroads into Asia Minor and the Balkans. Catalonia's amazing conquest of the Eastern Mediterranean was chronicled by Muntaner and early copies of his seminal work are conserved in the town's museum.

If you're a gourmand, the best time to visit this lovely little town is in summer, but for culture vultures it's charming all year round. The area's festes are suitably off season in November for the Festa Major de Sant Martí and in December for the Festa Major de Vilanova de la Muga. Both are relatively low-key and, whilst all the general festivities prevail, give a less bombastic view of Catalonia at play.

Ajuntament de Peralada, Plaça Gran, 7 Tel. 972 538 0 06 *www.peralada.org*

RIPOLL

Population: 10,832

What has always struck me about Ripoll is, despite its historical importance, its humble matter of fact atmosphere. It really comes across as nothing special, but this impression is totally false, and it's the town that can stake the strongest claim to being the 'Cradle of Catalonia'.

Ripoll's location where the rivers Ter and Freser meet on their way out of the Pyrenees means that it has a long history. During the Moorish invasion in the 8th century, most of the Catalan population had holed up in the mountains so the fertile spot that the town occupies was one of the first areas to be repopulated as the Saracens were driven south. In 888, Guifre el Pelós, the first hereditary Count of Barcelona, founded the Benedictine monastery of Santa Maria de Ripoll, which under Abbot Oliba was to become one of the foremost centres of learning in Europe.

The monastery itself is one of the finest examples of Romanesque architecture in existence, and is breathtaking in its simplicity. However, the real jewel in Ripoll's crown is the 12th century alabaster portal to the monastery, which was exposed to the elements for
132

800 years and fortunately is now protected by glass. The portal tells so many stories, both biblical and mythological, but can be seen as an allegorical description of the birth of the Catalan nation. Apart from going and just marvelling at this ancient piece of sculpture, it's well-worth picking up a free leaflet in order to get an idea of what it all might mean.

Ripoll's history has not been without its ups and downs. It has suffered from earthquakes and was particularly affected by the Carlist Wars, for example, but its fortunate location has always given it an air of modest prosperity. Consequently, it was well-positioned to take advantage of the Industrial Revolution, and this influx of wealth in the 19th century can be seen in the numerous Modernist buildings dotted around the town. One of the most charming of these is the tiny church of Sant Miquel de la Roqueta, built in 1912 by Gaudí collaborator Joan Rubió i Bellver, which looks like something out of Hansel and Gretel.

When you are in Ripoll, it's worth putting on the hiking boots and walking in the nearby mountains, and you should also take in nearby Sant Joan de les Abadesses, home to another Romanesque church and an extraordinarily well-preserved medieval centre.

Given Ripoll's importance in the Catalan psyche, it's not surprising that the town is host to some important festes. The Festa Major de Sant Eudald is held in mid-May and dates back to 1004, and in the following week there's the Festa Nacional de la Llana i Casament a Pagès, a festival that mixes sheep-shearing with traditional Catalan peasant weddings – it just can't get more authentic than this.

Ajuntament de Ripoll, Plaça de l'Abat Oliba, s/n Tel. 972 71 41 42 *www.ddgi.cat/ripoll*

The alabaster portal to Santa Maria de Ripoll is possibly the finest piece of Romanesque storytelling in existence.

This is what art critic Robert Hughes says about Ripoll in his seminal 'Barcelona'

'Cracked by fire, spalled by weather, battered by iconoclastic liberals, and now, fortunately, protected by a glassed-in porch, the alabaster façade of Santa Maria de Ripoll is the single greatest work of Romanesque sculpture in Spain. Even in its degraded state it remains mesmerizing, not only for the aesthetic vividness of its figures and emblems but for its narrative completeness. There are more than a hundred separate scenes... What is especially interesting about it ... is its power as a political statement. This is the earliest surviving Catalan work of sculpture to set forth metaphors of the foundation of Catalunya itself – the retreat of its people to the mountains and valleys before the Saracen armies and then the vision of return and the expulsion of the Moors. In the two... panels on either side of the entrance..., one sees the Biblical story of Exodus: Moses... the promised land, the rain of manna, the striking of water from the rock, the Israelites following... the column of fire... the removal of the Ark of the Covenant and the founding of Jerusalem, Daniel's vision of the Jews set free by the Messiah; and much more... For "Jews" read "Catalans"; for "Egyptians," "Saracens"; for "Moses,"... Guifré the Hairy; while the presence of ... Joshua (whose battle against Amalec at Rafidim takes up a large panel...) could only have been prophetic of the noble valor of the counts of Barcelona. And, of course, one also sees the Catalans working at their promised land: the inner face of the doorway arch bears scenes of labor, month by month – casting bronze in January, tilling in March, picking fruit in May, pruning in June, harvesting in July, butchering a deer in November, and so on.'

ROSES

Population: 17,173

Despite being one of the major resorts of the northern Costa Brava, Roses has a great deal going for it. During the high season it suffers from a predictable population explosion and it can be hard to find a space on the beach, but with 139 restaurants it's surprisingly well-equipped to deal with the mass of tourists, and is sufficiently large and historical for you to be able to find quiet spaces away from the madding crowds.

Roses is also about as solidly historical as you can get around these parts. Its location on the Bay of Roses meant that it has always been an attractive site for foreigners. The town was dubbed Rodes by the Greeks who founded it and its neighbour, Empúries, in the 8th century BC, and it was on this bay, only 30km south of the French border, that civilisation in Catalonia took its first steps.

The easiest way to get an idea of Roses' historical importance is to visit its impressive Renaissance Ciutadella. Inside you'll find remains of Greek and Roman civilisations and the Romanesque monastery of Santa Maria. Although these ruins are not quite as impressive as those at Empúries across the bay, they're certainly well-worth a visit. Further out of town you should also make time to see the Conjunt Megalíthic, which includes the dolmens Creu d'en Cobertella, el Llit de la Generala and el Cap de l'Home. These all date from around 3000BC and definitely give the idea that when the Greeks arrived, they weren't exactly settling in virgin territory.

Rather than doing all the history stuff, you could of course just stay on the beach, which is excellent. The town beach is of fine sand with a nice shallow incline into the water making it perfect for families with children. Outside the town towards the Cap de Creus

Nature Reserve there are lots of lovely coves that are ideal for diving and other water sports, which can be organised through a number of companies in Roses itself.

Finally, although the offers on food and drink in Roses are excellent, real foodies should take the road out to Port de la Selva and visit Ferran Adrià's world famous El Bulli restaurant. Unless you're royalty, you certainly won't get a table and even if you are it's not a foregone conclusion, so if you're really serious about sampling the food designed by possibly the world's most famous chef, I'd book now if I were you (*www.elbulli.com* Tel 972 150 457). Adrià's cooking breaks all moulds, and places food in the realm of both science and art. As he says himself, 'Cooking is the only creative work, other than sex, that uses the four senses: sight, smell, touch and taste. Think about it; when you look at a work of art you don't usually taste it or smell it. But the sensations that cuisine can give you are incredible.' I'm sure you won't be disappointed.

Ajuntament de Roses, Pl. Catalunya, 12 Tel. 972 25 24 00 *www.roses.cat*

The best preserved Greek ruins in Catalonia can be found at Empúries on the Bay of Roses.

TARRAGONA PROVINCE

It is not surprising that droves of tourists make a beeline for the Province of Tarragona every year. The obvious destination is the golden beaches of the Costa Daurada, but the region is much more than just sun, sea and sand. Tarragona itself is a wonderful city with more than 2,000 years of history – it was the Romans' first capital of Spain and it still houses the best-preserved Roman monuments on the Iberian Peninsula. Further south, the Ebro Delta nature reserve is a unique home to wildlife and a must for any ornithologist. Inland, there are vineyards, olive groves and the medieval villages that inspired Picasso to invent Cubism. You will also be delighted by the region's rich history – in the city of Tortosa, Christian, Jewish and Muslim communities coexisted for centuries and the castles in the area hark back to the time when the River Ebro was the frontier between Moorish and Christian Spain and the Knights Templar fought their Iberian crusades.

TARRAGONA

Population: 44,792

Tarragona is Catalonia's southernmost provincial capital, and thanks to its temperate climate, with an average yearly temperature of 23°C, its clean, sweeping beaches with their fine, golden sand and its singular artistic and architectural patrimony, officially declared a "World Heritage Site" by UNESCO, it is also one of the most delightful cities in the Principality. With Reus Airport just 7km away, and Barcelona a short 82km hop north, it's easy to get to. Moreover, Tarragona marks the junction of two major Spanish motorways, the Mediterranean Motorway, which runs from Alicante to France and the rest of Europe, and the Northern Motorway, which begins in Tarragona and runs through to the Basque Country.

The city itself divides clearly into two parts on two levels: the delightful High District, where you'll probably spend most of your time, and the Low District, which doesn't have quite so much going for it. Majestically sited on a rocky hill above the sea, the High District is an ancient place. Settled originally by the Iberians and then the Carthaginians, it was later used as the base for Scipio's march south against Hannibal in 218 BC and his subsequent conquest of the Iberian Peninsula, of which it soon became the capital. In 27 BC, Tarraco, the Roman name for Tarragona, briefly became the capital of the whole of the Roman Empire when Caesar Augustus made it his home.

Although Empúries is older, the Roman ruins at Tarragona are the most impressive in Spain.

139

Time spent in the High District quickly shows what attracted him to the city; it is beautifully and strategically located, and is now the site of the best-preserved Roman ruins on the peninsula and some excellent museums. It's also got an attractive medieval part, while the rocky coastline below conceals the first-rate Platja del Miracle beach. To get an idea of Tarragona's history, it's best to begin at the Passeig Arqueològic, a promenade that starts at Portal de Roser and encircles the northernmost half of the old town. The walk will take you along a path between the Roman walls, erected in the 3rd century BC, and the sloping outer fortifications, built by the British in 1707 to secure the city during the War of Spanish Succession. There are also remnants of the even earlier Iberian walls, Roman artefacts and 18th century British canons, and the vantage points often signalled by a telescope give fantastic views of the plain behind the city and the coast.

If your thinking of really getting under the surface of Tarragona's history, it's worth buying a Tarragona Card (24hrs - €12, 48hrs - €18, 72hrs - €24), which is available from tourist offices and gives you free entrance to the Passeig Arqueològic and the monuments and museums, which are definitely worth a visit. The Necropolis, Forum and Amphitheatre will take you back more than 2,000 years in time, while the Museu d'Historia and the Museu Arqueològic will explain Tarragona's historical importance.

The Tarragona Card also gives you free access to Tarragona's public transport, so you can visit other ruins slightly further afield, and also get down to the Platja Rabassada, which is where you might want to stay as it's an excellent beach backed by a couple of decent campsites. Another place you shouldn't miss out on is El Serrallo, the fisherman's district, where in the evening when the boats come in you can pick up excellent freshly caught fish.

As far as food and drink are concerned El Serrallo is an obvious choice, but there are first class restaurants all over the city with a great selection of fresh fish and seafood. Tarragona's fish has an official denomination, Peix Blau de Tarragona, which you should keep an eye out for. Tarragona's most emblematic dish is the cassola de romesco, a casserole based on a rich regional tomato and nut sauce, and every two years a contest is held during the Santa Tecla festivities to determine who makes the city's best. Seafood paella, as well as rice cooked in squid ink, grilled or fried fish, arrossejat (a rice and seafood blend simmered in fish stock), fideuejat (a seafood and noodle stew) and a wide assortment of creatively avant-garde recipes will also be on the menu.

City restaurants also draw on regional products brought from the local countryside, or Camp de Tarragona, including hazelnuts, almonds, oil and fresh vegetables, as well as meat and eggs. The nearby mountains add to this offer with wild mushrooms, potatoes and chestnuts, while the Ebre delta provides rice and citrus fruits. The select DO Tarragona wines also deserve special mention, in particular the mistelles and mellow dessert wines.

Many restaurants are housed either on the seafront or in historic buildings whose ancient Roman or medieval legacies can still be seen, transporting gourmands to an era of imperial splendour or the difficult years of the Spanish Reconquest. As an added flourish to this history-steeped setting, the month of May ushers in the "Tàrraco a Taula" food festival, where visitors can sample dishes made according to ancient Roman recipes.

If you visit the city in early spring, make sure you don't miss out on a calçotada, a kind of roasted spring onion party, where calçots are barbecued dipped in romesco sauce and people have competitions to see how many they can eat. I once ate 83, not a bad score, and then had to sit down for a three-course meal! If at all possible, go to a country restaurant with a group of friends, and you'll have a whale of a time.

The city beach is just one of the delights of Tarragona.

Other not to be missed events are Carnaval in late January/early February, Festivitat del Corpus, three days of religious events in early June, and Sant Joan on June 24th. The Festes Majors are Sant Magí, in the second week of August, and Santa Tecla, in the third week of September. In the first week of July, there's also an International Fireworks Competition (*www.pyroinfo.com*) and on October 1st, the city hosts one of the most important competitions in the Castellers calendar.

Ajuntament de Tarragona, Plaça de la Font, 1 Tel. 977 296 100 *www.tarragona.cat*. Permanent Tourist Offices are at Carrer Major 39 and Carrer Fortuny, 4, and seasonal ones on the Rambla Vella, Portal de Roser, Plaça Imperial Tarraco and a Kiosk on the Rambla Nova.

REUS

Population: 104,835

Reus is one of the undiscovered gems of Catalonia, which given that it's such a large town with its own airport is a little surprising. Most people just pass through on their way to the Costa Daurada, I suppose, but they really are making a big mistake. Reus has a gentle provincial quality all of its own, and with a thousand years of history behind it, it's an ideal base for discovering the whole of the province.

Its strategic position between the mountains and the sea makes Reus a great place from which to discover outstanding natural areas such as the Montsant massif, the Prades mountains or the Ebro delta. Reus also provides a starting point for fascinating tourist and cultural routes such as the Cistercian trail, including visits to the monasteries of Poblet and Santes Creus and the convent of Vallbona de les Monges, or to Roman Tàrraco. Reus is also just a stone's throw away from the Costa Daurada and its delights (sic). Sailing enthusiasts can find a host of marinas at their disposal and golfers have four courses within easy reach. After a hard day's serious tourism, you can come back to Reus to relax and stroll around the streets of the historic town centre and admire its fine Modernist heritage.

Reus, with a thousand years of history behind it, is an ideal base for discovering the whole of the province.

The origins of Reus lie in the mediaeval period, specifically in the 12th century, though it was not until the 18th century that the town's population grew so rapidly that it became the second most important town in Catalonia thanks to the liquor trade. The famous phrase "Reus, Paris, London" survives here as a reminder of this period of growth, recalling the fact that these were the three places where international liquor prices were set. Soon afterwards, in the late 19th and early 20th centuries, the fine Modernist buildings, which can still be seen today, were built.

Reus is famous for Gaudí, who was born in nearby Riudoms on 25th June 1852 into a family of coppersmiths, but spent his childhood and youth in the Reus. When he left for Barcelona at the age of 16, he never forgot the skills he learnt from the craftsmen in his hometown, and as some of his closest associates also came from Reus, including the architects Joan Rubió i Bellver, Domènech Sugranyes and Francesc Berenguer, Reus can claim its own highly influential school of art and architecture.

The arrival of Lluís Domènech i Montaner, the other great architect of the day, marked the beginning of the brilliant flowering of Modernisme in Reus. The year was 1898, and Domènech's first project was the Pere Mata psychiatric institute, which is considered one of the jewels of Catalan Art Nouveau. Lluís Domènech i Montaner's architectural style influenced other Modernist buildings, which went up around the town. His mark is clear in the work of the Reus architects Pere Caselles, Joan Rubió i Bellver and Pere Domènech Roura, the latter being Domènech i Montaner's own son. Due to the importance and distinctiveness of its Modernist heritage, Reus is part of the Art Nouveau Network, a European project made up of 14 towns and cities in 12 countries, the aim of which is to make the richness of their shared Art Nouveau heritage available to all.

Alongside Modernisme, Reus also has other important witnesses to its history. The 15th-century priory church of St. Peter, with its distinctive bell tower, is the most outstanding vestige of the old Reus and a symbol of the town. During the 18th and 19th centuries the town passed through a period of dramatic economic growth, which left its architectural mark in the form of three outstanding buildings: the Palau Bofarull (1770), the Centre de Lectura (1859) and the Teatre Fortuny (1882), one of Catalonia's leading theatres. Another essential part of getting to know the town is a stroll through the Plaça del Mercadal, the former market square, and the Plaça de Prim, veritable nerve centres of Reus life.

The celebrations in honour of Sant Pere, the town's patron saint, from 24th to 29th June, and for Misericòrdia (Our Lady of Mercy) from 21st to 25th September are excellent chances to discover the town's most deeply-rooted traditions and festivities. The Sant Jaume fair, one of the oldest in Catalonia, offers the chance to experience all the atmosphere of an evening fair in Reus.

On the menus of Reus restaurants, dishes originating in traditional cooking rub shoulders with those adapted from international cuisine. All of them are made using the finest Mediterranean ingredients such as Siurana extra virgin olive oil, a fruity, very mild oil, and the nuts which are so typical of the area, washed down with the wide range of excellent wines from the region's wine denominations: Priorat, Montsant, Terra Alta, Conca de Barberà and Tarragona. Without forgetting the famous vermouth of Reus.

In the Institut Municipal de Museus, Museu d'Arqueologia Salvador Vilaseca, the Museu d'Art i Història, the Centre de la Imatge Mas Iglesias and the Centre d'Art Cal Massó, Reus has got some great museums. The town is also home to Andreu Buenafuente and his band of brilliant comedians, El Terrat, so you'd better learn some Catalan to find out if the locals are taking the mickey or not.

Ajuntament de Reus, Plaça del Mercadal 1 Tel. 977 010 010 *www.reus.cat*

SALOU

Population: 22,096

If you're not put off by the fact that Salou's winter population of 22,000 reaches a peak of 180,000 during the holiday season, I'm sure you'll enjoy ten-minute train ride south from Tarragona through a gash of petrochemical pipes and tanks. Admittedly, once there, you'll be able to enjoy miles of golden sandy beaches, ringed around a sweeping bay and backed by a promenade studded with palms. From the seafront, it's quite an attractive prospect, but the town is resolutely downmarket with streets teeming with English pubs serving over-priced beer. Curries, Chinese and Fish and Chips are the culinary delights that can be sampled in Salou with its attempt to be a kind of Mediterranean Skegness.

Indicative of the cultural activities available in the town, the Ajuntament's website cites the Public Library as Salou's main area of interest. This is a shame because before it was overdeveloped for tourists in the 60s and 70s, Salou actually did have some history. During the 13th century, it was a major port, and it was from Salou that Jaume I the Conqueror's fleet set off on the conquest of Mallorca.

Culture and history, however, comes pre-packaged and prefabricated these days. Should you ever have the misfortune to experience a less than sunny day in Salou, you can always visit nearby Port Aventura (*www.portaventura.es*). Run by Universal Studios, Port Aventura is a theme park on a Disneyland Paris scale, which unlike its French counterpart doesn't suffer from bad weather and with more than half a million hotel beds in the vicinity is never short of visitors. People tell me that the rides, particularly Dragon Kahn are spectacular, and the themed areas cover things like the Wild West, Ancient China and other distinctly uninteresting topics. I

146

wouldn't be seen dead there, myself, but once again, I'm sure it's better than Skegness.

Ajuntament de Salou, Passeig de la Segregació, 4 Tel. 977309200 *www.salou.org*

TORTOSA

Population: 39,209

Located on the banks of the River Ebro, Tortosa is the main town and transport centre in the deep south of Catalonia, and an ideal place from which to explore the Ebro Delta and inland comarques such as Terra Alta. It's also a lovely town in its own right.

With more than two thousand years of history, there's a lot to see – Suda Castle and the Cathedral are fine examples of Gothic architecture but Renaissance and Modernist buildings are also well worth it. The city was originally a Celt-Iberian settlement that was later colonised by the Romans and then was one of the frontier towns between Christian and Moorish Spain in the 13th century during the reign of Jaume I the Conqueror. It actually was retaken from the Moors in 1148 by Ramon Berenguer IV, and it was because of its strategic position that it had to be fortified. These days it's much more peaceful, and Suda Castle includes a Parador de Turisme, a government-run hotel which although a bit pricey is an excellent place from which to take in the city.

The Cathedral is also a 14th century Gothic gem that includes more modern elements. The last time we visited was at Easter and we were privileged to be able to sit in on the rehearsals of the city choir for their big concert the following Sunday. As a matter of fact, Easter in Tortosa is one of the big events of the festival calendar and is not to be missed. Whilst inevitably being Christian in essence the celebrations include many Moorish and Jewish elements that hark back to the history of the city.

147

This mountain is in Terra Alta, a comarca in the Province of Tarragona, but is typical of the abrupt geography all over Catalonia. There's something I love about their Grail-like attraction.

Tortosa's multicultural origins are also reflected in its food, and the cake shops display sweetmeats that seem to combine Moorish, Christian and Jewish influences and are certainly not available anywhere else in Catalonia. According to my wife, the *pastissets* of sweet pumpkin and the small sugar and egg cakes called *garrofetes del papa* were particularly nice.

One of the nicest things about Tortosa is that it can all be done on foot. It's got a Jewish quarter, the city museum in the Església de Sant Domènech is particularly good and the Jardins del Príncep, which house a permanent open air exhibition of sculptures by Santiago de Santiago, are a delight. On a more sombre note, it's worth remembering that Tortosa is still very much a frontier town and is right on the southern border of Catalunya with the Comunitat Valenciana. In more recent times the city was on the frontline

148

between democratic and fascist Spain during the Spanish Civil war. 35,000 people died in the Battle of the Ebro and a haunting monument stands in the middle of the river as a commemoration to the lives that were lost defending a free and democratic Spain.

Apart from at Easter, the second half of June is a great time to visit Tortosa. First there's the Festes dels Reguers, then Sant Joan and on 24th June, the town celebrates the Festivitat de la Verge, which is the Festa Major.

Ajuntament de Tortosa, Plaça d´Espanya 1 Tel 977585800 *www.tortosa.cat*

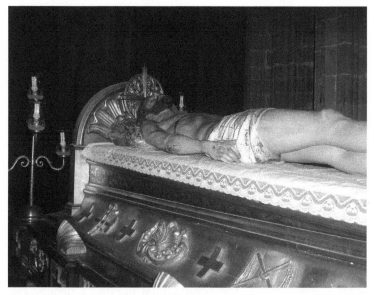

This picture of a prostrate Christ was taken in Tortosa Cathedral on the Thursday before Easter. A couple of days later he would be paraded through the streets during one of the most poignant Easter celebrations in Catalonia.

LLEIDA PROVINCE

Despite being the largest of the four Catalan provinces, the Province of Lleida is the least accessible and most difficult to define. The province is, however, full of history and mesmerising natural beauty, and given that it is completely inland, it has no coastline or beaches. This means that its many delights are completely off the conventional tourist track.

While Barcelona, Girona and Tarragona seem to follow relatively logical boundaries, Lleida Province is the clearest example of the fact that the Catalan provinces were imposed by politicians from Madrid in the 18th century. If you glance at a map of Catalonia, you will see that the north and south of the province have very little in common, and given that the provincial capital is in the extreme south, Lleida Province seems a rather strange name for this varied region. In fact, I would suggest that it would make a lot of sense to divide it into two – the Catalan Pyrenees Province in the north and Lleida Province in the south would be much more manageable.

The northern comarques of Val d'Aran, Pallars Sobirà, Alta Ribagorça, Pallars Jussà, Cerdenya, Alt Urgell and Solsonès are covered by the mighty snow-topped Pyrenees, which in winter months provide some of the best and most reasonably-priced skiing in Europe. For some strange reason, though, the idea of sitting in a ski station drinking gin and tonic whilst nursing a broken leg has never really appealed to me. However, roaming around the nature reserves with their lakes, peaks and prairies and then having a quiet beer in one of the medieval villages that hide awe-inspiring Romanesque architecture is quite a different matter.

This part of the world is deep-heart Catalonia and is just one of the nerve endings of the Catalan psyche that I seem to have tapped into. For more than two thousand years the Pyrenees have provided a frontier against invaders from the north and west but also a safe haven to hide out in when attacks came from the south or from the sea. Two thousand years ago even the Romans didn't manage to penetrate these mountain strongholds, and 700 hundred years later the Moors just came charging through on their way to the south of France. They decimated the fertile Catalan coastal plains, but within just a couple of decades the survivors were able to come down from the hills and repopulate their lands. This is why these tiny Pyrenean villages contain such ancient Romanesque churches. It is from here that the remaining Christians could push south and reclaim their territory.

Lleida province is full of history and mesmerising natural beauty but its many delights are completely off the conventional tourist track.

So, for both historical and geographical reasons, the Pyrenees are the core of Catalunya Vella, or Old Catalonia, and interestingly are much more accessible from the 'Old Catalan' provinces of Girona and Barcelona. The way the valleys connect to the sea means that it has always been much easier to get into the mountains from Ripoll in Girona Province or Vic in Barcelona Province than it is from the city of Lleida.

The south of the province is known as 'Terres de Lleida' or Lands of Lleida and is much flatter. This region is made up of the comarques of Noguera, Segarra, Pla d'Urgell, Urgell, Les Garrigues and Segrià, which is the southernmost comarca with the city of Lleida in its south-west corner almost touching on the rest of Spain. These rich agricultural plains are host to a very different kind of beauty and have a distinct story to tell. This is Catalunya Nova, or New Catalonia, and remained under Moorish control for nearly three centuries longer than the north. Consequently, its main architectural features are not secluded churches but mighty Templar fortresses that were built to hold the frontier. Furthermore, the fact that the Moors were there for much longer and that Lleida is still the conduit into the rest of Spain, providing the main road and rail links with Madrid, means that Northern Catalans view 'Lleidatans' with some suspicion. Even now, someone who speaks Catalan but comes across as rude and uncivilised can provoke the comment 'De Lleida ha de ser' – 'He must be from Lleida'!

This is probably unfair because the region is endowed with some beautiful gentle scenery and the Templar castles are truly breathtaking but, as someone who lives in Barcelona with family ties in Girona and French Catalunya, the Lleidatans do come across as being a little bit strange at times.

Diputació de Lleida: *www.diputaciolleida.cat*

LLEIDA

Population: 125,677

Lleida is the capital city of Segrià region and of the province that takes its name. Located on the River Segre in one of the most fertile areas in Spain, it is the most important population and economic inland centre in Catalonia and its strategic position means that if you're coming to Catalonia from Southern Spain by road or rail, you're almost certainly going to pass through Lleida. The city is particularly proud of the fact that it is linked to Madrid and Seville by the high-speed AVE train, which has only recently reached Barcelona.

Despite being a modern city with a University and particularly good shopping facilities, it is its history that particularly draws me. A settlement on the site goes back at least to the 6th century BC, when the Iberian tribe, the Ilergetes, established a fortified town called Iltrida on top of Roca Sobirana. Don't be misled into thinking that the Ilergetes were small cheese, because they managed to hold out against the Carthaginians and the Romans, who only finally sacked the town in 205 AD and changed its name to Ilerda. Roman chronicles describe a walled city with a stone bridge forming a municipality (founded in the time of Emperor Augustus) with fertile orchards, which, at the end of the 3rd century, were once again destroyed but this time by barbarian Germanic tribes.

View of the ancient city of Lleida.

In around 716, Lleida was occupied by the Saracens and the following four centuries of coexistence marked the character of the city. In October 1149, the Saracens surrendered to the troops of Ramon Berenguer IV, Count of Barcelona, and Ermengol VI of Urgell and Lleida became part of Catalunya Nova. Its position was of incredible strategic importance to Christian Catalans, and the Knights Templar were called in by the Counts of Barcelona to keep the marauding Saracens out of Catalonia.

The impressive Castell de Gardeny is the Templar command at Lleida, but the warrior monks were active all along the Southern Catalan frontier which ended at the Ebro Delta. Lleida is a great base from which to find out about this fascinating of history when the Catalan Counts and the Knights Templar essentially fought a European Crusade. A lot more information about what to see and do along with a lot of historical background can be found at *www.domustempli.com*

Many of the city's most emblematic buildings, for example the Palau de la Paeria and the Old Cathedral, date from these violent times, but architecturally Lleida has followed most of the trends typical of the rest of Catalonia since then. There are a number of 15th and 16th century churches and the New Cathedral is 18th century. If you're just passing through, the best way to get a quick overview is by taking a tour on the Bus Turistic, which costs about a euro and leaves hourly from Paeria/Pont Vell.

If you want to relax, Lleida has the privilege of being provided with natural areas such as La Mitjana nature park -an ecosystem of great natural and ecological value- the River Segre park and Camps Elisis. You are also almost within walking distance of the so-called Horta, an irrigated green belt that surrounds the city. In Lleida, lush greenery is never far away.

Lleida's two main festes take place in May and September and both last about a week. The Festa Major celebrates Sant Anastasi on 11th May, and is a typical Catalan street party with all its parades and celebrations. It's really worth catching a glimpse of the dragon, Lo Marraco, one of the symbols of the city and the oldest gegants in Catalonia, Marc Antoni and Cleopatra, which have paraded through these streets since 1840. Part of the festa is also taken up by the Festa de Moros and Cristians, a theatrical re-enactment of Lleida's Moorish past – not to be missed. The Festa de Tardor, the Autumn Festival, is in honour of Sant Miquel on 29th September and finally SENGLARock, on the last weekend in June, is establishing itself as one of Catalonia's prime rock festivals and is a great way to check out local talent.

Given its geographical proximity to fresh vegetables and meat, Lleida is a pretty damn good place to eat Catalan food with a slightly more exotic flavour (Moorish influence again). It also regards itself as the world capital for snail gourmets – if you can get past your prejudices, *cargols a la llauna* in their rich spicy sauce are truly delicious – if you're prepared to eat seafood, just think that a snail is just a mollusc on land – scrummy! Lleidatans refer to their own special style of cooking as 'Fruinar', good places to find out what this means are: Estel de la Mercè, Carrer Templers, 19 Tel. 973288008 or El Celler del Roser, Carrer dels Cavallers, 24 Tel. 973239070. But I suggest you just follow your nose!

Being such a large city there are plenty of places to stay in Lleida. A good option is the 3-star Catalonia Transit (Pl Ramon Berenguer IV s/n Tel. 973230008) in a magnificent building in the railway station or Hostal Mundial (Plaça de Sant Joan 4 Tel: 973242700) right in the heart of the city.

Ajuntament de Lleida, Plaça Paeria, 1 Tel. 807 117 118 *www.paeria.es*

LLEIDATANS ARE DIFFERENT

Although these days the Lleidatans allow their local government to be called the Ajuntament, in fact they still prefer the word Paeria. Furthermore, whereas in the rest of Catalonia the traditional title for the Mayor is *batlle*, which due to Castilian influence in recent years has become *alcalde*, in Lleida they stubbornly stick with the word *paer*.

PUIGCERDÀ

Population: 8,845

Situated high up in the Pyrenean comarca of the Cerdanya, Puigcerdà has a distinctly French feel. In fact, it is the capital of a comarca which once stretched well into France, much of which is now called Cerdagne and was lost to Catalonia after the Treaty of the Pyrenees in 1659.

Although it's a charming place with a very bourgeois café-bar feel and excellent shopping, there's not a lot to visit in Puigcerdà these days. The town was founded in 1177 but most of its historical heritage was destroyed as a result of the heavy bombing it suffered throughout the Civil War.

---

*The best thing about Puigcerdà is
the atmosphere of the place.*

One of the few monuments in the centre that survived the bombing was the forty-metre-high bell tower in Plaça de Santa Maria, and at the other end of town down the tree-lined Passeig de Deu d'Abril, which wasn't so heavily bombed, you'll find the church of Sant Domènec. This church is one of the largest in La

Cerdanya and despite its gloomy interior, it's worth visiting for its beautifully preserved medieval murals.

However, the best thing about Puigcerdà is the atmosphere of the place. If you've just arrived from France or are on you're way out of Catalonia, it's almost worth stopping the night here just to make the transition from one country to another. Lots of French trippers seem to think so anyway and the outdoor cafés in Plaça de Sant Maria or the adjacent Plaça dels Herois are great places to rest up for something to drink and eat. In the afternoon, you can always walk around the small manmade lake and admire the Modernist buildings.

Ajuntament de Puigcerdà, Plaça de l'Ajuntament s/n Tel. 972 880650 *www.puigcerda.com*

LA SEU D'URGELL

Population: 10,711

La Seu is up close to the border with Andorra, and provides an excellent base from which to explore the region if you don't want to go into Andorra itself. Once again, it's a town with a long history, and is named after its imposing cathedral on Carrer Major.

The cathedral is the seat of a bishopric that dates back to 820, and it was squabbles over land rights between the Bishops of La Seu d'Urgell and the Counts of Foix that led to Andorra gaining independence in the 13th century. The building itself wasn't consecrated until 1175 and has been restored several times since, but it contains some fine interior decoration and particularly lovely cloisters. As part of your visit, you should also go to the adjacent 11th century church of Sant Miquel and to the Museu Dioscesà, which contains a brightly coloured 10th century Mozarabic manuscript called the Beatus.

In reality, there's not much to see in La Seu but it's just an agreeable place to stroll about. There are some great bars along the dark, cobbled and arcaded old town streets in the area below the cathedral and there are some particularly fine 14th century buildings along Carrer dels Canonges.

If you're in La Seu, though, you're probably more interested in its surrounding area. For walkers Cadí-Moixeró Nature Park is a must, for those into water sports the Olympic facilities of the Parc Olímpic del Segre are another attraction and with four ski resorts nearby, La Seu is an ideal base for a winter sports holiday.

Ajuntament de La Seu d'Urgell, Carrer Portal de Cerdanya Tel. 973 350 010 *www.laseu.org*

TÀRREGA

Population: 16,100

Tàrrega is capital of the fertile Urgell comarca in the province of Lleida, and despite its size, its one of those places that that you seem continually driven towards if you're touring in southern Catalonia. Situated on the banks of the River Ondara between the Segarra and Urgell plains, it's also the meeting point for an extraordinary number of important roads; it's just off the A-2 motorway linking Barcelona, Lleida and Madrid, the C-14 from Tarragona and Montblanc up to Andorra passes close by and the Eix Transversal will take you all the way to Girona. Given that it appears you have no choice, it's probably worth stopping to have a look around.

Although very pleasant, Tàrrega doesn't figure very highly in the Catalan history books. It became populated after the Catalans won back Catalunya Nova from the Moors in the 12th century, but one of the highlights of its early career seems to have been 1458, when the town was given the right to hold a market on Mondays, which is still a cause for civic pride to this day and a very good to boot. The rest of its history is made up of plagues, minor skirmishes and the arrival of the railway. Apparently the bell tower of the church collapsed in 1672 destroying some local buildings, and the town's current hope for the future is the construction of the Segarra-Garrigues canal.

However, don't be put off by what little has gone on here because that's just part of its lazy charm. It's a lovely little place with a laid back atmosphere for 11 months of the year, and should you visit in September, Tàrrega explodes into life. Every year it hosts the Fira de Teatre al Carrer, the Festival of Street Theatre, which is absolutely fantastic. There are shows in the street, in bars, in community centres and sometimes even in private houses. More than 100 theatre groups come from all over Europe, but the great thing is that local Catalan amateurs come and put on shows just for the hell of it; buskers, mime artists, clowns, break dancers. Anyone with a fun idea can set up in Tàrrega and do their show for free. You can get information about the official programme at *www.firatarrega.com*, but I suggest you just turn up with a guitar or a set of juggling clubs.

Ajuntament de Tàrrega, Plaça Major, 1 Tel. 973 311 608 *www.ajtarrega.es*

Essential Information

CRIME

Crime is not a particular problem, so unless you're very unlucky keeping safe is a question of common sense. Just like in the rest of Europe, the larger towns and cities have 'no-go' zones where it is not advisable to walk around on your own late at night. The backstreets at the lower end of the Rambla in Barcelona, for example, are haunts for drug addicts and muggers. Tourist areas, public transport, Internet cafes, ATMs and hotel lobbies are also common hangouts for pickpockets and petty thieves.

Pickpockets are rarely violent, but you do have to watch out for some common scams. Beware of someone who tells you you've got something on your shirt and offers to clean it off for you, as they will also be cleaning out your wallet at the same time. Other scams include the mock football game when a group of boys kick a football your way and when you join in crowd around you and pinch your wallet, the 'Got a light?' routine when as your giving a light to one person an accomplice removes your wallet, and of course there's the standard bag snatch, which is sometimes perpetrated by kids on motorbikes.

Another recent disturbing trend has been a spate of violent burglaries on the luxury housing estates near the Costas. If we're to believe the newspapers, houses have been broken into in the early hours of the morning, and organised gangs of Eastern Europeans have bound and gagged victims and withdrawn money on credit cards during the following day. Police vigilance has been stepped up in these hitherto safe havens, but if you're wealthy enough to own such a property, it's really a question for your insurance company and a security expert.

If you're a victim of a crime you must report it to the local police, which will be either the Policia Nacional or the Mossos d'Esquadra, the autonomous Catalan police, on 091 or 092 depending on where you live. The situation of the police is a little confusing in Catalonia at the moment as the Policia Nacional are in the process of handing over responsibility for crime investigation to the Mossos d'Esquadra, whilst the Guardia Urbana, the municipal traffic police, are responsible for traffic. The final force, the Guardia Civil, who were particularly powerful under Franco, are less visible in Catalonia than in the south of Spain.

HEALTH

There are no particularly common health problems in Catalonia, unless you count sunburn and hangovers, both of which are best cured by resting indoors and drinking lots of liquids. EU nationals with a European Health Insurance Card (EHIC) can consult a National Health Service doctor free of charge. Any prescribed medicines can be bought at the pharmacy at prices set by the Ministry of Health. Nevertheless, adequate medical insurance is always a good idea.

In Catalonia, the pharmacist is an important figure in the health care chain and sells drugs over the counter that would require a prescription in Britain. For minor ailments you can simply explain your symptoms to the pharmacist and he or she will probably be able to help you. If not, he or she will give you the address of the nearest doctor or in towns and tourist areas, Centre d'Assistencia Primaria (CAP). CAPs are local health centres containing a number of doctors' surgeries and normally a *metge de guardia*, a standby service, where you will be attended after a short wait. For a medical emergency, most large towns have hospital with Urgencies (A and E departments) or you can call 112 or 061 for an ambulance.

DRIVING

The best way to discover Catalonia's nooks and crannies is by car, and valid drivers' licences from most countries are recognised if you're driving as a tourist. However, with no Park and Ride system, driving can be a nightmare in cities and in the twisted streets of tiny Catalan towns, and although drivers are a little less aggressive than in southern Spain, they are considerably more pushy than the British. Tempers flare particularly during the rush hours (7.30-10am and 7-9pm) and on Friday and Sunday evenings when everyone is heading out of town or coming back from a weekend away, and the roads and motorways are clogged with traffic.

Another problem can be finding a place to park depending on where you are and what time of year it is. In Barcelona it's always difficult, but in the off-season parking in most small towns and coastal resorts is easy and generally free. In peak season on the coast and in Barcelona all year round, it's worth budgeting upwards of €20 a day to leave your car at a parking metre or in a multi-storey car park. The latter are signalled by a large blue 'P' sign and are often cavernous underground places with parking spaces so small that it's almost impossible to get out of your car.

Just as in the rest of mainland Europe, road signs follow EU regulations and drivers drive on the right, so traffic regulations regarding giving way and overtaking are a mirror image of British conventions. Speed limits are

120kph (75mph) on major highways, 80kph (50mph) on secondary roads and 50kph (31mph) in cities and towns. A few years ago, speed limits were not strictly enforced but the introduction of speed cameras and a points system for driving infractions has meant that the police's attitude has got a lot tougher recently. Similarly, permitted blood alcohol levels are extremely low in Catalonia compared to most of the rest of Europe, breath checks are routine, especially in areas known for their nightlife.

Most of the major car rental firms operate in Catalonia, including Hertz (*www.hertz.com*), Europcar (*www.europcar.com*) and Avis (*www.avis.com*), which all have offices in Barcelona and at the airport and Sants Estació, the major railway station. If you have car trouble or a breakdown you should contact RACC (*www.racc.net*), the Catalan automobile club or contact your own service in Britain, which will probably send RACC to attend you anyway.

Rental Car Links

www.hertz.com
www.europcar.com
www.avis.com
www.racc.net

SHOPPING

With home-grown industries in ceramics, textiles, shoes, olive oil, cured sausages and wines and some great clothes and jewellery designers, Catalonia is a particularly good place for shopping. To get an idea of what's on offer it's worth paying a visit to the mega-department store El Corte Inglés (*www.elcorteingles.es*), which has branches all over Catalonia, but it's a lot more fun to rummage around and find interesting items close to the places they are made.

Although you'll have no problem in big shops, in the smaller ones you'll be expected to pay in cash as Catalans have a particular aversion to credit cards. One of the advantages of this is you might get offered the item *sense rebut*, without a receipt, making it an unofficial sale, which means you shouldn't have to pay the 16% IVA (VAT).

If you want to buy Catalan-made ceramics, the best place to head for is La Bisbal d'Empordà, a few miles inland from the northern Costa Brava, or in Barcelona visit Art Escudellers at Carrer Escudellers, 2. For fuet and butifarra, traditional Catalan cured sausages, Vic is the undisputed capital, but its fine products can be found in xarcuteries and tocineries all over Catalonia. Wines and olive oils – look out for DO Siurana from El Priorat – are similarly ubiquitous.

Learning to dress like a Catalan is one of the challenges of coming here, so let's keep it simple and start with your feet. For comfy but stylish shoes you could try Camper (*www.camper.es*), which has shops all over Catalonia, the one at Rambla de Catalunya, 122 being the closest to the centre of Barcelona, or for something a little more refined Farrutx (www.farrutx.es).

If you want to be really hip and pick up on next year's thing, you should check out Catalonia's up and coming designers Custo Barcelona (*www.custobarcelona.com*), Armand Basi (*www.armandbasi.com*), Lydia Delgado, Josep Font (*www.josepfont.com*) and Antonio Miró (*www.antoniomiro.es*) to name but a few. For even more interesting clothing, in Barcelona you can window shop in the area around Santa Maria del Mar and El Born or the Plaça del Pi, and for international names like

Emporio Armani, Chanel, Max Mara and Gucci your best bet is Passeig de Gràcia or Avinguda Diagonal.

Shopping Links

www.elcorteingles.es
www.camper.es
www.farrutx.es
www.custobarcelona.com
www.armandbasi.com
www.josepfont.com
www.antoniomiro.es

A CATALAN PHRASEBOOK

A FEW PRONUNCIATION RULES

The Catalan Language is Català to its people, and as a general rule tends to use the throat, back of the tongue and front roof of the mouth much more than the very lippy and tonguey Castilian pronunciation – Spanish comedians often make good use of this when they perform skits on the Catalans. For this reason, you should not be tempted to apply any Spanish pronunciation rules you might know. This is particularly true of the soft Z and C sounds, so unlike in the rest of Spain, the natives do not pronounce Barcelona as Barthelona but rather Barsselona – that long sibilant 's' is very Catalan.

When Manuel in Fawlty Towers used to say 'My name ees Manuel, and I com from Barthelona', actor Andrew Sachs was getting it completely wrong.

Here's an overview of some more basic sounds:

- A as in 'cat' if accented, as in 'America' if unstressed eg. the middle A in Català
- E varies and is often pronounced as in 'get', but also like the A in America
- I as in 'police'
- IG sounds like 'tch' as in 'pitch' eg. 'boig' (mad) is pronounced 'botch'
- O is normally pronounced as in 'hot'
- U is somewhere between 'put' and 'rule'
- UI as U above in 'Puig' (pronounced 'putch') or 'oo-ee' as in 'fruita'
- Ç sounds like an English S, so plaça is pronounced 'plassa'
- C as in 'cat' if followed by A, O or U, as in 'sat' if followed by E or I
- G as in 'go' unless followed by E or I when it is pronounced liked ZH in 'Zhivago'
- H is always silent
- J is like the sound in the French name 'Jean' but a little harsher
- L and L.L are pronounced as in English
- LL is similar to the double L in 'million'
- NY replaces the Castilian Ñ
- QU before E or I sounds like K and is pronounced as in 'quick' before A or O
- R is rolled at the start of a syllable but like in English is often unpronounced at the end of a word
- V and W sound like B at the start of a word
- X is like SH in most words but sometimes sounds like X as in 'exit'
- Z is like the English sound in 'zoo'

Basic Expressions	Spanish	Catalan
Yes, No, OK	Si, No, Vale	Si, No, Val
Please, Thank you	Por favor, Gracias	Si us plau, Gràcies
Where, When, What	Donde, Cuando, Que	On, Quan, Què
How much, How many	Cuanto/a, Cuantos/as	Quant/Quants/Quantes
Here, There, Over there	Aquí, Allí, Allá	Aquí, Allà, Més enllà
Now, Later	Ahora, Después	Ara, Després
This, That	Esto, Eso	Això, Allò
Open, Closed	Abierto, Cerrado	Obert, Tancat
Good, Bad	Bueno, Malo	Bo, Dolent
Big, Small	Grande, Pequeño	Gran, Petit
Cheap, Expensive	Barato, Caro	Barat, Car
Hot, Cold	Caliente, Frío	Calent, Fred
More, Less	Mas, Menos	Més, Menys
Today, Tomorrow	Hoy, Mañana	Avui, Demà
Day before yesterday	Antes de ayer	Abans d'ahir
Next week/ month/year	La semana/el mes/el ano que viene	La setmana/el mes/l'any vinent

Meeting People	Spanish	Catalan
Hello, Goodbye	Hola, Adiós	Hola, Adéu
Good morning	Buenos Días	Bon dia
Good afternoon	Buenas Tardes	Bona tarda
Good night	Buenas Noches	Bona nit
See you later	Hasta luego	Fins després
Sorry	Lo siento	Ho sento
Excuse me	Perdone	Perdó
How are you?	¿Como estas?	Com estàs?
I (don't) understand	(No) entiendo	(no) entenc
You're welcome	De nada	De res
Do you speak English?	¿Hablas ingles?	Parles anglès?
I(don't)speak	No hablo	No parlo
Spanish/Catalan	español/catalán	Espanyol/català
My name is...	Me llamo...	Em dic...
What's your name?	¿Como te llamas?	Com et dius?
I'm English/Scottish	Soy inglés/escocés	Sóc anglès/escocès
Welsh/Irish	galés/irlandés	gal·lès/irlandès
American/Canadian	estadounidense/ canadiense	estadounidenc/ canadenc

Hotels	Spanish	Catalan
Do you have a room free?	¿Tiene una habitación libre?	Té una habitació lliure?
For one night	Para una noche	Per una nit
For two people	Para dos personas	Per dues persones
With a shower	Con ducha	Amb dutxa
What time can we have...?	¿A que hora podemos...?	A quina hora podem...?
Breakfast/lunch/dinner	Desayunar/comer/cenar	Esmorzar/dinar/sopar
Could you wake me at...?	¿Me podría despertar a... ¿	Podria despertar-me a... ?
The bill, please	La cuenta, por favor	El compte, si us plau

Transport	Spanish	Catalan
How do I get to...?	¿Como llego a...?	Com vaig fins a ...?
Where is...?	¿Donde está...?	On és...?
I'd like a (return) ticket to...?	Quiero un billete (ida y vuelta) para...?	Voldria un bitllet (anada i tornada) per...?
What time does it leave?	¿A que hora sale?	A quina hora surt?
The underground	El metro	El metro
The airport	El aeropuerto	L'aeroport
The train station	La estación de trenes	L'estació de trens
The bus station	La estación de autobuses	L'estació d'autobús

Numbers	Spanish	Catalan
One	Uno/Una	U/Un/Una
Two	Dos	Dos/Dues
Three	Tres	Tres
Four	Cuatro	Quatre
Five	Cinco	Cinc
Six	Seis	Sis
Seven	Siete	Set
Eight	Ocho	Vuit
Nine	Nueve	Nou
Ten	Diez	Deu
Eleven	Once	Onze
Twelve	Doce	Dotze
Thirteen	Trece	Tretze
Fourteen	Catorce	Catorze
Fifteen	Quince	Quinze
Sixteen	Dieciséis	Setze
Seventeen	Diecisiete	Disset
Eighteen	Dieciocho	Divuit
Nineteen	Diecinueve	Dinou
Twenty	Veinte	Vint
Twenty one	Veintiuno	Vint-i-un/una
Thirty	Treinta	Trenta
Forty	Cuarenta	Quaranta
Fifty	Cincuenta	Cinquanta
Sixty	Sesenta	Seixanta
Seventy	Setenta	Setanta
Eighty	Ochenta	Vuitanta
Ninety	Noventa	Noranta
A hundred	Cien	Cent
Two hundred	Dos cientos	Dos-cents
A thousand	Mil	Mil

Days, Months, Seasons	Spanish	Catalan
Monday	lunes	dilluns
Tuesday	martes	dimarts
Wednesday	miércoles	dimecres
Thursday	jueves	dijous
Friday	viernes	divendres
Saturday	sábado	dissabte
Sunday	domingo	diumenge
January	enero	gener
February	febrero	febrer
March	marzo	març
April	abril	abril
May	mayo	maig
June	junio	juny
July	julio	juliol
August	agosto	agost
September	septiembre	setembre
October	octubre	octubre
November	noviembre	novembre
December	diciembre	desembre
Winter	Invierno	Hivern
Spring	Primavera	Primavera
Summer	Verano	Estiu
Autumn	Otoño	Tardor

Please note that the days of the week and months are not usually written with a capital letter in either Spanish of Catalan.

Emergencies	Spanish	Catalan
Help!	! Socorro!	¡Socors!
I am ill	Estoy enfermo	Estic malalt
I am hurt	Estoy herido	Estic ferit
The hospital	El hospital	L'hospital
A doctor	Un medico	Un metge
A pharmacy	Una farmácia	Una farmàcia

Restaurant	Spanish	Catalan
Table reserved	Mesa reservada	Taula reservada
Set Menu	Menú del día	Menú del dia
Menu	Carta	Carta
Fork	Tenedor	Forquilla
Knife	Cuchillo	Ganivet
Spoon	Cuchara	Cullera
Teaspoon	Cucharita	Cullereta
Glass	Copa/Vaso	Copa/got
Plate	Plato	Plat
Apple	Manzana	Poma
Bread	Pan	Pa
Butter	Mantequilla	Mantega
Chicken	Pollo	Pollastre
Duck	Pato	Ànec
Egg	Huevo	Ou
Fish	Pescado	Peix
Fruit	Fruta	Fruita
Grape	Uva	Raïm

Restaurant	Spanish	Catalan
Ham	Jamón	Pernil
Cooked ham	Jamón York	Pernil dolç
Ice cream	Helado	Gelat
Lamb	Cordero	Xai
Mustard	Mostaza	Mostassa
Omelette	Tortilla	Truita
Orange	Naranja	Taronja
Pastry/cake	Tarta/pastel	Pastís
Peach	Melocotón	Préssec
Pepper	Pimienta	Pebre
Pork	Lomo	Llom
Potatoes (baked, fried, boiled)	Patatas (al horno, fritas, hervidas)	Patates (al forn, fregides, bullides)
Rabbit	Conejo	Conill
Rice	Arroz	Arròs
Salad	Ensalada	Enciam
Salt	Sal	Sal
Sausage	Salchicha	Salsitxa
Sugar	Azúcar	Sucre
Tomato	Tomate	Tomàquet
Veal	Ternera	Vedella
The bill, please	La cuenta, por favor	El compte, si us plau
Service included	Servicio incluido	Servei inclòs

Resources

NEWSPAPERS & MAGAZINES
In The UK
www.livingspain.co.uk - Living Spain
Tel. 00 44 01234 710992

www.aplaceinthesunmag.co.uk - A Place in the Sun
Tel. 00 44 01737 786 800

www.livingabroadmagazine.com - Living Abroad Magazine

Tel. 00 44 0131 226 7766

In Spain

Catalonia Today
www.cataloniatoday.info

Metropolitan
www.barcelona-metropolitan.com - Barcelona

Costa Brava Resident/Costa Daurada Resident
www.creativemediagroup.es

Catalunya Life
www.catalunyalifeonline.com

Think Spain
www.thinkspain.com

La Vanguardia
www.lavanguardia.es

El Periódico de Catalunya
www.elperiodico.cat

Avui
www.avui.cat

RECOMMENDED READING

Barcelona – Robert Hughes (Vintage ISBN 0 679 74383 9): This anarchic irreverent history of Catalonia covers all the major events with the added plus that Hughes, as an art critic, gives profound insights into the genesis of Catalan style, design and architecture.

Homage to Barcelona – Colm Tóibín (Picador ISBN 0 330 37356 0): An almost poetic impressionistic view of Catalonia. Tóibín is particularly good at bringing the magic of Catalan festivals to life.

The Basques, the Catalans and Spain – Daniele Conversi (Hurst & Company ISBN 1 85065 268 6): Apart from giving an overview of Catalan and Basque history from the 19th century to the present, Conversi examines why the Basque cause turned to violence whereas the Catalans chose the road to democracy.

Homage to Catalonia – George Orwell: 'Homage to Catalonia' (Harvest Books ISBN 0 156 42117 8 is an essential read for anyone who wants to do more than scratch the surface of the Catalan psyche. As a member of the International Brigades during the Civil War, Orwell took part in gun battles on Les Rambles and fought on the Aragonese front. He would later reinterpret his experiences in Catalonia in 'Animal Farm' and '1984'. For a parallel vision of the Civil War in Catalonia, Ken Loach's film 'Land and Freedom' is also well-worth watching.

The City of Marvels – Eduardo Mendoza (Pocket Books ISBN 0 671 70234 3): This wonderful novel tells how Onofre Bouvila, a low-life crook at the International Exhibition of 1888, transforms himself into a respectable businessman for the the second International Exhibition of 1929. Along the way there is intrigue, violence and much Machiavelian manoevreing – a brilliant look at turn of the century Barcelona.

The Shadow of the Wind – Carlos Ruiz Zafón (Phoenix Fiction ISBN 0 75382 120 6): This international bestseller paints a dark romantic mysterious Barcelona – perhaps not always a true reflection of the city but an absolutely fantastic read.

MORE LINKS

A complete and up-to-date list of web links to estate agents, language learning resources, hotels, travel companies and other useful contacts for visitors and investors in Catalonia can be found at *www.nativespain.com*

About Simon Harris

I arrived in Barcelona in April 1988 in search of adventure and a change in my life. I was soon playing in rock bands and teaching English. I met my wife a year after my arrival and our daughter was born in December 1994. I currently teach English in the Servei de Llengües of La Universitat Autònoma de Barcelona.

A BARCELONA STORY

Barcelona's main streets were lined with trestle tables piled high with books, and gypsy girls peddled red roses from every street corner. It was April 23rd 1986, El Dia de Sant Jordi, the Catalan equivalent of Valentine's Day and I was on holiday in Barcelona with an American girlfriend.

Flushed by the romance of the moment, I bought her a rose on the Rambles and then we looked at books. As they were all in Catalan or Spanish, I decided that music would be an adequate substitute, in keeping with the spirit of the day of the book and the rose. So we wandered in and out of side streets, before finally finding a record shop on Carrer Tallers, where she bought me a Gypsy Kings cassette.

The day was hot and sweaty and we had been trudging around for ages, so once we were back at the top of the Rambles, I was gasping for water. I saw a large ornate iron drinking fountain, and I stopped to quench my thirst. What I did not know at the time was that this was the Rambla de Canaletes, and there is a legend that says that anyone who drinks water from the fountain will always return to Barcelona.

The holiday came to an end and I returned to London, but by the spring of 1988 as legend predicted, I was back for another holiday. My brother was in Barcelona taking a couple of years out after university, and I was tired of trying to make it as a musician in London. So it was not difficult to persuade me that the holiday could be extended. English teaching would pay the rent, and my original idea was just to spend a year enjoying myself – with no plans. I was open to anything and everything, prepared to let life take me wherever it wanted me to go.

My brother was living in an amazing flat overlooking El Mercat de Santa Catalina in the heart of the Ciutat Vella, the old city. It was so primitive it was almost prehistoric. The building had an old wooden door with an enormous iron knocker. He lived on the fifth floor so you had to bang the door, as hard as you could, five times. The problem was, though, that it was impossible to be heard over the street noise generated by the market, so the only way to get in was to shout until you were hoarse. If anyone was home they would finally let you in by hauling on a metal chain connected to a medieval latch inside the door. Then you walked up five storeys in pitch darkness and finally arrived at the attic, sweaty and exhausted. I had a place to stay, though, and its lack of modern conveniences made those first few months in Barcelona all the more authentic.

My Spanish was nonexistent, but as most of the people I met were foreigners, just passing through, it didn't really matter. I soon learned to ask for beer and for cheese bocadillos, so I had the basics covered. I was also having the time of my life – beaches, bars and parties, and Barcelona was just a great place to have fun. It struck me as a kind of rundown Paris, just as architecturally impressive when it wanted to be, but somehow much more rough and ready – more comfy and welcoming, I suppose. I set about exploring the city in earnest, and was aware that the history of the city seemed to be told by the names of its streets – Ausiàs Marc, Consell de Cent, Bruc, Via Laietana. I had no idea what these names referred to, but somehow they conjured up a magical past that fired my imagination.

It was late spring 1988, and it was a great time to be footloose and fancy free. I spent most of my time with other foreigners who were just as intent on enjoying themselves as I was. So when my brother and most of the people I had met moved on, over the summer, I was left alone with a rudimentary grasp of Spanish and a strong sense that there was little point in making friends with people who would soon be leaving. I think it was then that I also began to notice other foreigners' negative attitudes to the Catalan language.

Obviously, for all of us, it made sense to concentrate on Spanish – we had got no idea how long we were going to stay, and for me at least, a good grasp of it might open up the doors to a few years travelling in South America. But perhaps because I had reasonably good working knowledge of French, my attempts at making myself understood often led me to use Catalan words for things. 'Farina' for flour seemed more obvious than 'harina', as did 'formatge' rather than 'queso' for cheese. It was obvious to me even then that Catalan had more in common with French than it did Spanish. One only had to look at the similarity between 'Si us plau' and 'S'il vous plait', and when we were out drinking the fact that my Catalan friends asked for 'una birra' rather than 'una cerveza' seemed much easier – particularly after you had consumed a few of them.

However, I was working at my Spanish, and nobody expected me to do anything else. People even translated street names into Spanish. I know they were just trying to be helpful, but it could be very confusing at times. I once got invited to a party – 'Calle Fernando just off The Ramblas,' I had been told. I started my search at the top of The Rambles – Santa Anna, Canuda, Portaferrissa, Cardenal Casañas, Ferran, Escudellers. I walked all the way down and there was no sign of it. I tried the other side – Santa Mònica, Nou de la Rambla, Unió, Hospital. As I was having no luck, I went for a drink on the terrace of Glaçiar in Plaça Reial feeling a bit sorry for myself. Luckily, I ran into some people who were also going to the party. 'Calle Fernando is Spanish and Carrer Ferran is Catalan', they laughed as we downed our beer and left. How was I supposed to know?

You also have to remember that this was 1988, and Franco's dictatorship was still very much alive in the minds of Spanish and Catalans alike. During the regime, the dictator had tried to obliterate the Catalans' collective memory of their own history by changing the names of the streets. I was aware that Diagonal for example had been called La Avenida del Generalísimo for forty years and had only recently changed back. Similarly, most people referred to Plaça Francesc Macià as Calvo Sotelo, but one day I was called for interview for a teaching job uptown. 'Get off at Metro Entença, walk up the street and you'll see a sign for the school diagonally opposite when you get to Infanta Carlota.' Once again I walked about like someone who had just landed on Mars. Finally, I asked someone, who fortunately took pity on me and took me right to the door. 'But this street is Josep Taradellas,' I said. 'They only changed the sign a couple of years ago,' was the reply. 'Everyone still calls it Infanta Carlota.' Despite hoots of laughter at the school, they were very understanding and gave me the job.

The names of the streets, then, seemed to tell two conflicting stories, and I resolved to find out more. Another conflict that seemed crucial to the people was centred on football. 1988 was a great time to be English in Barcelona. Terry Venables had recently managed Barça, and Gary Lineker was the star accompanied by Steve Archibald and Mark Hughes. I, needless to say, became a fan, in part because reading about football in the local newspapers was a lot easier than politics.

I used to go to a bar in the Barri Gòtic to watch the games. The great thing about Bar Lopez, or Santi's as I used to call it, was that they had two televisions. Santi Senior supported Real Madrid so the telly next to the bar always showed the Madrid game, whilst Santi Junior was a Barça fan, which meant that you could always watch 'el equip blaugrana' in the back room. On football nights, I actually managed to find myself a position where I could watch two games at once – pure heaven.

Perhaps where I decided to sit, though, meant that I really had not taken sides yet, but it did give me the chance to observe the different ways in which the two groups reacted. Madrid's goals were celebrated with 'Olé' and flamenco twirls, whereas when Barça scored the tables were hit in a way that was full of restrained aggression and pride. The Catalans reaction was less attractive than that of the Spanish, but much closer to how I naturally reacted myself. If a goal was missed or a game inexplicably lost, the back room was full of frustrated expletives – 'Collons… Me cago en Déu.'

'Me cago en Déu' soon became an unanalysed part of my vocabulary. I, like my fellow Barça fans, used it to express frustration at their lack of scoring ability, but it also came in handy when the Metro arrived late or when

I suspected I had been overcharged in one of the late-night bars around my Plaça Reial stamping ground. It probably took me about six months to stop and think about it word for word. This came in a kind of Eureka moment, I had in the presence of a couple of rather gorgeous hippy girls whilst sitting outside Glaçiar in Plaça Reial. I knew the expression also existed in Spanish, but overhearing them talk to each other in Catalan, I was stopped in my tracks... 'Me cago' – I shit... 'en Déu' – on God... 'Me cago en Dèu' – I shit on God? What an extreme concept. In English the word 'shit' is bad enough on its own without mixing it up with blasphemy. Other swearwords like 'De putamare' were just as shocking. It is used to mean absolutely fantastic but literally it would be translated as 'Of whore-mother' – a guttural reference to the perfect woman who opens her legs and irons your clothes as well... and I was hearing these words coming from the lips of two apparently well-brought up university students. Culture shock!

The fact that the Catalans suffered from a scatological obsession also hit me in the face quite early on. I remember going to see the nativity scene on display in Plaça Sant Jaume just before my first Christmas in Barcelona. It was presented so beautifully – Jesus' birth with low level lighting, life size figures of Mary, Joseph, the shepherds and the kings. But at the back was a figure of a man dressed in traditional Catalan costume with his trousers down. He was bent double and the product of his efforts, exquisitely modelled in fibreglass, lay below his bare bottom. For me, this was another moment when what I was experiencing did fit in to the world as I had been taught to see it. What on earth was he doing there? Was it some kind of Dalí-esque joke?

Nothing could be further from the truth - this was El Caganer, an important pillar of the Catalan psyche. He is 'The Shitter' who fertilises the ground, and is even present at the birth of Christ, arguably the most significant moment in modern history. What is even more amazing is that he is regarded as a normal and necessary part of the Nativity Scene displayed in almost every Catalan household over the holiday period, and in some circles caganers are collectors' items.

Along similar lines is 'Caga Tió' – the shitting log, which is the centrepiece of pre-Christmas children's parties. Children go up in turn and hit the log (which normally has a face painted on it) with a stick. Angelic boys and girls can be heard shouting 'Caga, caga, caga' – 'Shit, shit, shit' – and presents are expelled, as if by magic, from under a tablecloth that covers its backside. I am sure Freud would have a lot to say about this.

I was picking up a sense of these people, but only loosely aware of how they described themselves, which is in terms of 'rauxa' and 'seny'. The latter of these, 'seny' is the attribute that the Catalans like to sell to the outside world as their public face, and a very rough approximation is common sense. At the same time, though, it is fair play, amicable reserve and looking before you leap.

When I arrived in 1988, the idea of 'seny' seemed to be embodied by Jordi Pujol, the president of the Generalitat, Catalunya's governing body. He was a conservative middle-class ex-banker who was now running the country. He had been arrested during the Franco regime for promoting Catalan culture and language, but was moderation incarnate, capable of pacting with the Castillian right as long as what they had to offer fitted in with his Catalan nationalist game plan.

Rauxa is the yang to seny's yin, and provides a balance to the Catalans' hard-working mercantile character. It is unbridled passion that can easily turn to moments of excess, and, as I was on a long-term holiday, I was intent on enjoying all the rauxa the city had to offer. Crossing Plaça Reial from the terrace of Glaçiar to the hot sweaty ambience of Karma, the most happening disco in town. Late night forays into the backstreets of the Casc Antic. The cultured decadence of El Nus, the Latin American vibe of the glass-fronted bars along Passeig del Born. Always winding up drunk, out of order but happy at 5 o'clock in the morning in one of the bars where the stallholders breakfasted behind my local market, Mercat de Santa Catalina.

Although I had no idea of what it meant my life was guided by a kind of happy holiday rauxa, that I only became aware of on the night of Sant Joan, Midsummer's Eve. It was so amazingly crazy. We went for a few beers in the barri and then took the metro up to Plaça Espanya around eleven, freezing cold bottles of cava tucked under our arms. Corks were popped before we hit the street, which was alive with the smell of gunpowder. Rockets and bangers exploded around us, people dragged us into mad dances. We slugged on our cava exchanging bottles with whomever we came across. People hugged us and offered tokes on their spliffs. I can only remember thinking that in Britain this would be termed public disorder but here it meant joyful happiness, uncontrolled freedom and let's party. What a paradigm shift that first Sant Joan was for me!

Although run by the civic authority, El Ajuntament, Barcelona's annual city festival, La Mercè, held in September also has its moments of rauxa. The Catalans' obsession with fire is exemplified in the Correfoc. This is rauxa with seny. There is a procession of demons called diables through the streets each person setting off a splendid firework at a given time. The impression is wild but everything stays just this side of total chaos, so amazingly no-one gets hurt.

The focal point of La Mercè, as it is with so many cultural events, is Plaça Sant Jaume which is the historical heart of Barcelona, and therefore, of Catalunya. In the years I lived in the Barri Gòtic, I went there on Sunday evenings on a regular basis. Why? Because, on Sunday nights in Plaça Sant Jaume, people dance the Sardana.

Amongst the foreigners I knew, the Sardana was treated as a bit of a joke, perhaps because it is not as explosive and passionate as flamenco, they always saw it as an example of how boring the Catalans were. I did not agree. There is something I find innately attractive about seeing a group of musicians sitting on a small raised wooden platform making acoustic music for people to dance to. And, in actual fact, the Sardana is full of musical complexities, subtleties and eccentricities. The wind instruments are primitive and harsh on the ear, every piece begins with a wild whistle introduction and then a Boom-Bu-Bu-Boom bass, which could almost be heavy metal, kicks in. The tunes and harmonies float from major to minor chopping, at least to the incogniscienti, inexplicably between 4/4 and 6/8.

Even the dance itself balances the complex and the absurdly simple. The dancers form circles that can be as small as five or six people but can grow to include fifty as new dancers arrive. Depending on the rhythmic thrust of the section, there are two steps, and these circular movements are danced almost like individual ripples within the larger collective circle. The dancers raise their hands and move their feet while the caller, usually an elderly man, signals changes in the music by pressing the palm of the person next to him. Within in moments the message has been passed along to all the dancers and everybody changes step on time. It seems to me an incredible example of cooperation and communication; seny in action.

If I had to summarise Catalan culture with just a few images it would be a close choice between the Circle - sardana dances, the castellers' human castles and these Catalan children's shoes.

Another folkloric practice also particular to Catalunya, as far as I know, are castells. I first saw these human castles during La Mercè in Plaça Sant Jaume but they are celebrated all over Catalunya. There are three parts to the castle – 'la pinya' or base, 'el tronc' or trunk and the 'pom de dalt' or crown of the castle. Watching them being put together is an amazing and inspiring sight, and the first time I saw it brought tears to my eyes.

At the base, a group of thirty or forty strong men lock forearms, shoulders and heads in what appears to be a disorganised rugby scrum. Four more big men climb on top of these and lock forearms in a circle. Four lighter men now climb up the tower and do the same. There then may two more floors of yet lighter people often adolescents – girls are not excluded. By this time, the castell may be as high as ten metres, and those at the top are a long way from the ground. Legs begin to wobble and brows start to show the strain, but up goes a child of nine or ten who forms an arch over the top pair. Finally, the anxaneta, a tiny child of five or six scales the castle. All the adults look up ready to catch if, as often happens, the tower crumbles and falls. The tension can be cut like a knife, but finally the youngster hitches his or her way right to the top, raises an arm and the castell is counted as valid. Everybody comes down as quickly and safely as they can. The kids are met by hugs and kisses from their proud but distraught parents, whilst the burly men exchange manly embraces with their equally burly companions. It is a moment of victory and emotion, and if this is not an amazing example of what an amazing people are capable of achieving through trust and working together, tell me what is.

I think by the end of that first Mercè I was already addicted to quite a lot more than Barcelona's beaches and bars, but it was not until a few months later, when I bought myself a black and white portable TV that I was sold hook, line and sinker.

In those days there were two public channels and perhaps one or two commercial ones in Spanish. To be perfectly honest, most of the time all that was on offer was absolute rubbish – dreadful South American soap operas, endless quiz shows and surreal 'live from Murcia' variety galas where the producers seemed to think that they could make up for the performers' lack of talent by draping scantily clad women over them. I had not even bothered to tune in to TV3, the only

Catalan channel, because I feared it would be just as bad, and even worse I would not be able to understand it. But when I did, lo and behold, there was Star Trek - The Next Generation translated into Catalan. 'Espai, l'última frontera... aquests son els viatges de la nau estel.lar Enterprise.'

I began to watch Catalan TV on a regular basis, which was great for my passive understanding of the language, and soon discovered that apart from the excellent homegrown documentaries and news programmes, there seemed to be a British connection which, given that I was deliberately trying to avoid foreigners, served to ameliorate my enyorança or homesickness. The Young Ones, Fawlty Towers, Some Mothers Do 'ave 'em and Yes, Minister were all dubbed into Catalan. I must admit the first effect was a little surreal, but as I had seen most of the episodes before, I soon got used to it. It also struck me even then that the Catalans' criteria were closer to mine than those of the Spanish, as the only British comedy series on Spanish TV was The Benny Hill Show.

Round about the same time, we started getting Eastenders, Coronation Street and Neighbours in Catalan, which although not great art were a lot better than the South American soaps shown on Spanish TV. I have always believed that these series left their mark on Catalan TV. Current Catalan soaps like El Cor de la Ciutat, set in my home barri of Sant Andreu, are difficult to dislike while Spanish TV continues to import South American junk and anything it produces itself is so inane as to be unwatchable. Similarly, Catalan comedy, stand-up comedian Andreu Buenafuente or the sit-com, Plats Bruts, being obvious cases in point, has a distinctive intelligence and an upmarket feel that makes it curiously addictive.

So, after a year, I was beginning to understand something about my new home. Then something happened that would make the legend of Canaletes come true. I met my wife and, suddenly, I was part of a Catalan family and later, when my daughter was born, I became a Catalan in all but birthplace.

I seemed to have no choice but to go in search of the real story behind this people. I know they don't consider themselves a 'lost nation' but even now, most foreigners come with the idea that they are visiting Barcelona, Spain and are unaware of the vibrant culture, the mighty language and their extraordinary imperial history. Yes, Catalunya is part of the Spanish state, but search for it and you'll find that it's much, much more than that.

CAN SIMON HELP YOU FURTHER?

I have a very full life and a very consuming, but satisfying, job teaching English at the University. This means that I have three months free over the summer which I can dedicate to 'creative' projects. I would be happy to take on further guides/book projects and literary or simultaneous translations. I am also available to give guided tours of Barcelona and Catalonia or provide linguistic consulting. I can be contacted through my profile at *www.nativespain.com*.

NativeSpain™.com

Be in our next guide...

We're committed to ensuring the quality of our guides
and as such have set up a free membership site for readers
and natives to share their hot tips and updates...

Find out all about Spain's towns, cities,
culture, beaches, restaurants and more.

Use the diary feature to share your story, as it unfolds,
with other expats and would-be expats in Spain. Learn
from other people's successes and mistakes in the forums.

Join FREE, get involved and you could be
featured in one of our printed guides...

Write your own guide...

We're in the process of creating Native's guides o all
regions of Spain. If you're an expat now living in a new part
of Spain and have a skill for writing then get in touch with
us to find out more about author opportunities...

www.NativeSpain.com

We look forward to welcoming you
to our growing community!

"What the guidebooks failed to tell you about living, working and investing in Spain."

NativeSpain.com

Spain

2008 *the expat survival guide*

Yolanda Solo

"if you live in Spain you need this book"

www.nativespain.com

A BRIT'S SCRAPBOOK

GOING NATIVE IN MURCIA

SECOND EDITION

The Essential Guide for Visitors, Expats & Homebuyers

MARCUS JENKINS
DEBBIE JENKINS

FREE FLIGHTS TO BE WON

www.nativespain.com

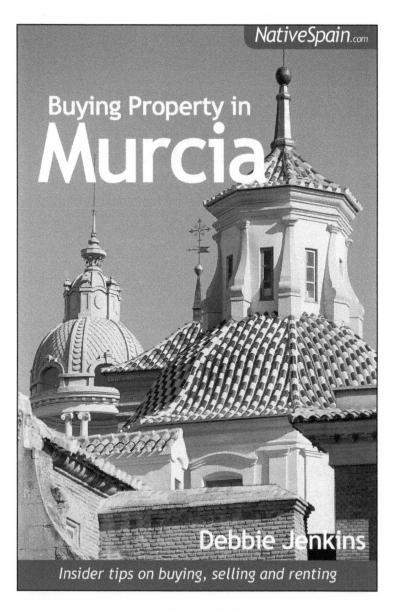

NativeSpain.com

Buying Property in
Murcia

Debbie Jenkins

Insider tips on buying, selling and renting

www.nativespain.com